Improve Your English Writing

Kenneth A. Wick

Improve Your English Writing
(November 2021 Revision)

Copyright © 2021 by Kenneth A. Wick

Table of Contents

Introduction

People notice grammar mistakes and awkward sentences in essays, term papers, emails, letters, reports, presentations, sales material, social media posts, and other material.

College courses and the global economy require top-notch writing skills.

In college, superior writing skills result in higher grades and a better chance of hearing "you're hired" after graduation. A survey of employers showed 73 percent want to hire someone with strong writing skills, and it ranked third behind leadership ability and teamwork for the most desired skills.[1]

At work, superior writing skills lead to success and career mobility. According to a 2019 *Forbes* article, a person's writing ability is the "most important skill in business."[2] An effective writer moves up the career ladder while a weak writer is passed up and left behind by co-workers and competitors.

Are your writing skills holding you back from higher grades, finding a job, or career mobility?

According to the *Forbes* article, writers must know the "rules" to write well. *Improve Your English Writing* will teach you the superior writing skills needed to improve grades and to increase career opportunities. This book is a how-to manual of the most important and frequently used writing rules.

Superior writing produces **clear, concise,** and **correct** sentences. Clear writing is easy to understand. Concise writing is to the point, not wordy. Correct writing follows the grammar, punctuation, and formatting rules of a popular style guide (rule book), like *The Chicago Manual of Style*.

---

[1] Kaleigh Moore, "Study: 73% of Employers Want Candidates with This Skill," published April 7, 2016, *www.inc.com*.
[2] Jeff Bradford, "Why Writing Ability is the Most Important Skill in Business (and How to Acquire It)," published January 29, 2019, *www.forbes.com*.

The writing rules in *Improve Your English Writing* are not my rules and guidelines. They are the writing rules and guidelines from the most popular style guides:

- *The Chicago Manual of Style* for books
- *The Associated Press Stylebook* for newspapers
- *The Gregg Reference Manual* for business
- The *MLA Handbook* and APA manual for academic writing.

Important rule differences are noted when the style guides disagree, allowing a person to follow a specific style guide.

Because *Improve Your English Writing* cannot cover everything, it utilizes the Pareto Principle (80/20 rule). This means roughly 80 percent of superior writing comes from 20 percent of the writing rules. *Improve Your English Writing* contains the writing rules that produce superior writing.

Abbreviations:
The following abbreviations are used throughout *Improve Your English Writing.*

Abbreviation	Source
AP	*The Associated Press Stylebook 2019*
APA	*Publication Manual for the American Psychological Association* (7th Edition, 2020)
CMOS	*The Chicago Manual of Style* (17th Edition, 2017)
GRM	*The Gregg Reference Manual* (11th Edition, 2011)
MLA	*MLA Handbook* (9th Edition, 2021)
MW Dictionary	*Merriam-Webster.com Dictionary* (Approximately 240,000 entries. Accessed December 2020.)

Improve Your English Writing is dedicated to my wife, Ellie.

Purpose and Audience

All writing has a purpose and an audience. It could be an email to a co-worker (audience) about a customer complaint (purpose), a term paper on the late 2000s Great Recession to an economics professor, or an advertisement for a new brand of toothpaste for potential consumers.

Purpose:
The purpose is always known.

Audience:
Write to the audience. The audience determines content, word choice, and organization. For example, a student writes about the late 2000s Great Recession in a term paper to an economics professor and in an email to an interested friend. While the student's purpose is the same, the content, word choice, and organization will differ because of the audience.

Content:
Base the necessary content on the audience's knowledge and understanding. Often a lengthy and detailed explanation is not required. Too much content or explanation may keep the reader from focusing on the purpose, and too little content or explanation may create questions in the reader's mind. Confusing content requires reorganization or rewriting.

Word Choice:
Writing for co-workers or specialists in an academic field will likely contain industry jargon or technical language. Use words the audience understands.

For example, a government engineer receives an email from a resident about the terrible pavement condition of their street. In an email to a co-worker, the engineer writes the roadway's Pavement Condition Index is thirty-five. This is technical jargon. The reply to the resident contains language they understand: the pavement is in "poor" condition.

<u>Organization:</u>
Good document organization improves clarity. A popular format in academic journals is abstract, introduction, method, results, and then discussion. However, the introduction–body–conclusion format is well known and dominates writing.

Introduction:
State the purpose in the introduction. The introduction may grab the audience's attention or explain why the purpose is important.

Body:
The body fulfills the purpose stated in the Introduction. Common ways to organize the body include:

- **Argument from General to Specific**. Follow a general discussion with specific information or examples. Include counter-arguments, if necessary, to strengthen the argument. Many people are familiar with this format.

- **Argument from Specific to General**. Specific information or examples build to a general discussion. This format works best when the ideas in the general discussion are less popular.

- **Problem-Solution**. Discuss a problem and then present one or more solutions. Organize multiple solutions by best first, best last, cost, or another method.

- **Chronological**. Arrange the examples or information by time or sequence.

- **Best Reason Last**. Arrange the reasons or information in increasing order of importance.

- **Degree of Familiarity**. Arrange the information from most to least familiar. This format works best with a list of reasons, causes, or effects.

- **Degree of Complexity**. Arrange the examples or information from the least to the most complex. The audience will begin with fundamental information before progressing to more complex information.

- **Spatial**. Group the information by "area" for a place or thing, such as survey results, a car repair manual, or an architectural review of a building.

- **System-by-System**. Group the information by "system," such as automotive systems, physiology systems, or U.S. government branches.

- **Pros and Cons**. Group the information by advantages (pros) and disadvantages (cons).

Conclusion:
The conclusion does not thoughtlessly end the document. It answers, What should the audience take away after reading the document? A good conclusion accomplishes the following:

- **Restates the purpose**. Do not simply copy the purpose from the introduction. Word the conclusion differently while echoing the introduction. One technique uses a vivid image that represents the purpose or its implications.

- **Summarizes**. Summarize the key points. One technique uses a compelling example that expresses the key points.

- **Recommends a Course of Action** (optional). The conclusion may recommend a course of action or include a call to action.

The Three-Step Writing Process

The three steps of writing are

1. **Outlining**. Connect and organize ideas into a list of points arranged in writing order.

2. **Writing the First Draft**. Express the outline with imperfect paragraphs and sentences.

3. **Editing**. Rewrite and correct the first draft.

Outline:

An outline improves clarity. It organizes ideas and key points into something the audience can understand, and it saves time during writing and editing. An outline is either formal or informal.

An informal outline lists the key points in writing order. Use it for simple documents, like emails or short essays. A formal outline lists the key points and subpoints in writing order. Use it for longer documents, like reports or term papers.

Indent formal outline levels symmetrically. Try to limit the levels to three or fewer because an audience may have difficultly following more levels. Use Roman numerals (I, II), then capital letters (A, B), and then numbers (1, 2). When creating or editing a list of subpoints, use two or more subpoints. Revise the outline or move the subpoint when a level has only one subpoint.

Informal Outline
(email on policy change):

Old Policy Summary
Reason for Change
New Policy Summary
Employee Training

Formal Outline
(new policy):

I. Background
   A. Old Policy Summary
   B. Reason for Change
II. New Policy
   A. New Procedure
   B. Exceptions
      1. Exception 1
      2. Exception 2
III. Required Employee Training

Creating an outline for an email is simple and fast. Developing an outline for a term paper or long report requires more time and effort. **Do not skip the outlining step**. Outlining saves time when writing the first draft because it reduces the "what do I write next" time. Create an outline by

1. Writing the purpose.
2. Brainstorming and listing points.
3. Adding, editing, combining, or deleting points.
4. Organizing the points into key points and subpoints.
5. Arranging the key points and subpoints in writing order.
6. Repeating steps 3 to 5 as necessary.

First Draft:

The first draft is the initial expression of the outline with imperfect paragraphs and sentences. Do not fear writing awkward sentences and grammatical errors because no author has yet produced a perfect first draft. Write freely knowing the clunky sentences and other mistakes will be corrected during editing.

The saying "**Don't get it right, get it written**" is true. Because writing is the primary goal of the first draft, below are some tips for staying laser focused on writing.

- **Remove Distractions**. Turn off the cell phone and close the internet browser.

- **Start Anywhere**. Writing does not automatically begin with the introduction. Begin with the easier-to-write portions based on knowledge or preference.

- **Write Freely**. Write what comes to mind. Be receptive to new ideas, insights, and connections.

- **Keep Writing**. For writer's block, write a description of the needed text, highlight it, and move on. Circle back to it before finishing the first draft.

- **Limit Editing**. The first draft must focus on writing. If necessary, set brief time limits for editing.

- **Take a Break**. Take a periodic break. Write for fifty minutes followed by a ten-minute break.

The sentence is the fundamental unit of writing. *The Chicago Manual of Style* and other writing guides categorize English sentences into four types: simple, compound, complex, and compound-complex. Knowing these sentence types helps an author create better and correct sentences.

Consult Appendix A for unfamiliar grammatical terms or for a grammar refresher. Understanding independent and dependent clauses is especially important.

<u>Simple Sentence:</u>
A simple sentence consists of one independent clause and no dependent clauses. A sentence may begin with a coordinating conjunction (usually *and* or *but)*, but do it sparingly.

- She kicked the ball.
- I gave him money for a loan.
- And Kendall arrived five minutes early.

<u>Compound Sentence:</u>
A compound sentence consists of two or more independent clauses and no dependent clauses. Two independent clauses may be separated in the following three ways (using *I went to the grocery store* and *I saw a friend from high school*):

1. A comma and a coordinating conjunction.
   If either independent clause contains a comma, consider using a semicolon between the clauses (see page 67).

   - I went to the grocery store, and I saw a friend from high school.
   - I went to the grocery store and bought eggs, milk, and bread; and I saw a friend from high school.

2. A semicolon without a coordinating conjunction.
   The independent clauses should be closely related (see page 66). If they are not closely related, separate the independent clauses with a period.

   - I went to the grocery store; I saw a friend from high school.

8

3. A semicolon, a conjunctive adverb (or transitional expression), and a comma.
   Do not place a comma after the conjunctive adverbs *hence, then, thus, so*, and *yet*. A period may be used instead of a semicolon.

   - I went to the grocery store; consequently, I saw a friend from high school.
   - I went to the grocery store; thus I saw a friend from high school.

Separating three or more independent clauses in a single sentence is the same as separating a series of three or more items (see page 62). However, a sentence with three or more independent clauses is normally too long for reading comprehension. Limit a sentence to only two independent clauses (see page 29).

<u>Compound Predicate</u>*:*
Do not confuse a compound sentence with a simple sentence containing a compound predicate. A compound sentence has two subjects and two predicates. A simple sentence with a compound predicate has one subject that shares two predicates.

- Lucas visited Brazil and stayed with his family.
  - The two predicates, *visited Brazil* and *stayed with his family*, share one subject: *Lucas*.

- I went to the grocery store and saw an old friend from high school.
  - The two predicates, *went to the store* and *saw an old friend from high school*, share one subject: *I*.

Do not separate the compound predicates with a comma unless it adds clarity or prevents a misreading.

- Maria noticed the real murder who entered the court room, and gasped.
  - The comma clarifies Maria gasped, not the murder.

<u>Comma Splice and Run-On Sentence</u>:
A comma splice occurs when only a comma separates two independent clauses. The coordinating conjunction is missing.

- Our teacher graded the homework, several students received perfect scores.

A run-on sentence occurs when two independent clauses have no punctuation between them.

- Our teacher graded the homework several students received perfect scores.

The above run-on sentence example could be written in the following ways:

- Separated into two sentences.
  - Our teacher graded the homework. Several students received perfect scores.

- Separated with a comma and coordinating conjunction.
  - Our teacher graded the homework, and several students received perfect scores.

- Separated with a semicolon.
  - Our teacher graded the homework; several students received perfect scores.

- Separated with a semicolon, a conjunctive adverb (or transitional expression), and a comma.
  - Our teacher graded the homework; shockingly, several students received perfect scores.

<u>Complex Sentence</u>:
A complex sentence consists of one independent clause and one or more dependent clauses. A dependent clause may be joined to an independent clause in three ways:

1. Independent clause followed by an essential dependent clause.
   No punctuation separates the clauses.

   - I broke my thumb before I took my summer vacation in Hawaii.

2. Independent clause, comma, nonessential dependent clause.

- I broke my thumb in January, before I took my summer vacation in Hawaii.

3. Dependent clause, comma, independent clause.

- Before I took my summer vacation in Hawaii, I broke my thumb.

<u>Compound-Complex Sentence:</u>
A compound-complex sentence consists of two or more independent clauses and one or more dependent clauses. The rules for combining them are the same as compound and complex sentences. If either independent clause contains a comma, consider using a semicolon between the independent clauses (see page 67).

- I broke my thumb before I took my summer vacation in Hawaii, but the doctor said I would be able to snorkel with a special covering over my cast.

- Before I took my summer vacation in Hawaii, I broke my thumb, but the doctor said I would be able to snorkel with a special covering over my cast.

- Mary, who is my cousin from Idaho, is visiting me this weekend; and I hope she is not allergic to cats.

Edit:
Writing the first draft may be an achievement. Therefore, pause and acknowledge how much was accomplished.

The focus now shifts to editing. Some people do not want to hear that much of editing is rewriting. The good news is the clunky, error-filled first draft will transform into something far superior through rewriting and polishing those sentences.

Editing produces clear, concise, and correct writing. Clear writing is easy to understand. Concise writing is to the point, not wordy. Correct writing follows the grammar, punctuation, and formatting rules of a popular style guide, like *The Gregg Reference Manual*.

The Copyeditor's Handbook and *The Chicago Manual of Style* discuss different types of editing.

- **Developmental Editing**. Developmental editing focuses on the overall document content and organization through adding, removing, structuring, reorganizing, displaying, and presenting the content.

- **Substantive Editing**. Substantive editing improves clarity and conciseness by rewriting unclear or wordy sentences, reorganizing sentences, and reworking the content or presentation of tables and graphs.

- **Mechanical Editing**. Mechanical editing formats the writing to a style guide's rules for grammar, syntax, word usage, punctuation, spelling, capitalization, number formatting, and so on. Popular style guides include *The Chicago Manual of Style* for books, *The Associated Press Stylebook* for newspapers and magazines, and *The Gregg Reference Manual* for business.

- **Copyediting**. Copyediting includes both substantive editing and mechanical editing. *The Copyeditor's Handbook* states, "copyeditors are expected to make simple revisions to smooth awkward passages, [but] copywriters do not have the license to rewrite a text line by line." Therefore, a copyeditor does mechanical editing and light substantive editing. When major substantive editing is required, the document is sent to a substantive editor or back to the author.

- **Proofreading**. Editors work with the prepublication document call a "manuscript." When editing is completed, the publisher converts the manuscript into an electronic or hard copy publication format called the "proof." A proofreader works with the proof before actual publication and focuses on typesetting and formatting errors introduced during the conversion from manuscript to proof. A proofreader also corrects any mechanical edits missed during copyediting.

The Three-Step Editing Process

For many documents, the needed revisions cannot occur in a single editing pass. Therefore, edit the document in the following order to maximize productivity:

1. **Document Organization and Order.** Focus on developmental editing by revising the document's overall content and organization based on the outline. Also, revise paragraph order and content, including sentence order.

2. **Intense Sentence-Level Edits.** Focus on substantive editing by revising bulky or awkward sentences for clarity and conciseness.

3. **Sentence-Level Polish.** Focus on mechanical editing by revising sentences for correct grammar, syntax, word usage, punctuation, spelling, capitalization, number formatting, and so on.

Editing not completed in this order results in needless rewriting and polishing. Why spend time crafting an awesome sentence if the content is not needed? Likewise, why spend time properly punctuating an unclear or long-winded sentence that needs rewriting?

Edit in passes where each pass targets something specific. When the focus of an editing pass is too broad, clunky sentences and grammar errors will remain. Few people, however, have time to make numerous editing passes due to a deadline or editing fatigue.

The two best editing plans are the three-pass and five-pass editing systems. Both deliver good bang for the buck. Unless the document is short, doing less than three editing passes will likely leave too many grammatical errors and poorly written sentences. Doing more than five editing passes leads to diminishing returns, yielding few revisions for the required effort.

Three-Pass Editing System:
The three-pass editing system is the recommended minimum editing effort. It is best for documents with fewer than fifty pages.

The first editing pass focuses on revising the document's overall content and organization using the outline as a guide. Rewriting some awkward sentences may occur, but most revisions should be to the document's content and organization.

The second editing pass focuses on rewriting unclear or wordy sentences. Reorganizing a few sentences and correcting some punctuation may occur. However, most changes (80 percent or more) should be sentence-level changes focusing on clarity and conciseness.

The third editing pass focuses on "polishing" sentences. Rewriting a few slightly awkward sentences may occur. Most edits should be related to grammar, word usage, punctuation, capitalization, number formatting, and so on.

Five-Pass Editing System:
The five-pass editing system is best for documents with fifty or more pages. It is the three-pass system with the second and third pass repeated twice.

The first editing pass focuses on the document's content and organization. The second and third passes focus on intense sentence-level edits for clarity and conciseness. The fourth and fifth passes focus on sentence-level polishing for grammar, punctuation, and so on.

Document Organization and Order

Editing begins with reviewing and revising the outline. Change it based on necessary content, document organization, and any ideas or comments received while writing the first draft.

Next, focus on the overall document. Write missing content, delete unnecessary content, rearrange sections of related text, and move tables and graphics.

Finally, focus on paragraphs. Rearrange paragraph order within sections of related text. Then revise paragraph content by rearranging sentence order.

Content:
Content editing is straightforward: remove the unnecessary information and add any missing information. Too much content typically results from over-explanation, and the reader becomes lost in a jungle of details or examples. Remove unnecessary details and use the best examples. Too little content, however, may leave the reader with questions. The missing reasoning, details, or examples must be added.

Do not add "padding" while writing the first daft. For example, you need to write a twenty-page term paper. You write nineteen pages and have nothing else to add. Therefore, you pad the term paper to twenty pages by adding unneeded sentences and empty phrases to existing sentences. Bad idea.

Editing removes padding because superior writing is concise writing. Plan to lose 5 to 10 percent of the document length or word count while editing for clarity and conciseness. Therefore, if an assignment is to write a twenty-page term paper, write at least twenty-two full pages before editing.

Clarity:
Clarity means directly stating the purpose or the purpose is obvious. Directly state the purpose in the introduction, and restate it using original words in the conclusion.

Good document organization improves clarity because it logically presents the information. Because many people are consciously or subconsciously familiar with the common methods of document organization, clarity is built-in. Common methods include introduction-body-conclusion, argument from general to specific, problem-solution, and chronological (see page 4).

Paragraphs:
A paragraph, a group of related sentences, improves clarity because all sentences have the same topic. The average paragraph contains four to eight sentences (75 to 150 words).

Short paragraphs may lack details, reasoning, or examples that support the paragraph's topic. Long paragraphs often contain too much detail, unnecessary examples, or stray from the paragraph's topic. Consider breaking a very long paragraph containing detailed or multiple examples information into separate paragraphs.

Paragraph length varies based on the form of writing. Newspapers and websites have shorter paragraphs, and academic documents have longer paragraphs.

Sections:
A section is a group of related paragraphs that might follow a section heading. Websites and long documents often contain section headings that allow a reader to scan the content.

Section headings usually mirror the outline levels. Just as each outline level is symmetrically indented, use an identical font style (regular, boldface, underline, italic) and alignment (center, left, run-in) for each section heading level. Section headings should also use parallel and consistent wording. Some style guides, like the *American Psychological Association* (APA), specify the formatting.

Section Level	Gregg Manual (Recommended)	APA (Required)
1	Center, Capitalized Boldface	Center, Boldface
2	Left, Boldface	Left, Boldface
3	Run-In, Boldface	Left, Boldface Italic
4		Run-In, Boldface
5		Run-In, Boldface Italic

Section Level	Recommended
1	Center, Boldface
2	Left, Boldface
3	Left, Underline
4	Left, Italics
5	Run-In, Italics

Tables and Graphics:
A table or graphic (diagram, pie chart, bar chart, or line graph) efficiently presents a large amount of data. A table shows how raw data compares or contrasts. A pie chart shows the relationship of parts to a whole, a bar chart compares data groups, and a line chart often compares data over time.

According to *The Copyeditor's Handbook*, a table or graphic answers two questions: "What specific purpose is this item intended to serve? and Is this particular item the best way to serve that purpose?" These two questions address clarity. The table or graphic's purpose is obvious, and the information is presented in an easy-to-understand way.

Intense Sentence-Level Edits

After revising the document's content and organization based on the outline, edit each sentence focusing on clarity and conciseness. Also, verify every sentence is one of the four sentence types, reworking it as needed. Do not waste time fussing over the grammar or punctuation because the sentence may be rewritten. Some adjusts to the document's content and organization may be needed, but these changes should be minor.

A person will read over errors while self-editing because the brain supplies the "correct" version instead of the error. Use the following tips for sentence-level edits:

- **Allow Time Between Editing Passes**. Give the brain time to forget—the longer, the better. Work on something else if possible.
- **Read Slowly**. Slowly read and re-read each sentence. Break it down into clauses and phrases, and analyze each sentence element.
- **Change the Font Size**. By rearranging the text, the brain's chance to read over errors decreases.
- **Take Breaks**. Take a periodic break. Edit for fifty minutes followed by a ten-minute break.

Clarity:
A clear sentence is easy to understand. An unclear sentence may contain a cliché, weak verb, misplaced adverb, or overused sentence type.

<u>Keep Related Words Together:</u>
English depends on word order for meaning. A reader expects the subject first, the verb second, and any objects third. The reader also anticipates an adverb or adjective will be placed next to the word it modifies.

Consider the sentence: *dog bites man*. *Dog* is the subject, *bites* is the verb, and *man* is the object. What does the biting (dog) and who gets bitten (man) is determined by the word order. Now consider the sentence: *man bites dog*. The reversed word order has the opposite meaning.

Exceptions to subject, verb, then object word order include questions where the verb may come first (Is Tammy working today?), commands where the subject is omitted (Stop that!), and passive voice (see page 25).

Place an adjective (big) or adverb (falsely, precisely) next to the word it modifies: big ship, falsely accused, calculate precisely. An adjective is almost always placed before the noun it modifies, and thankfully a misplaced adjective is uncommon. Depending on the situation, an adverb is placed before or after the verb, adverb, or adjective it modifies. An adverb answers the how, where, when, or why about the word it modifies.

Determining if a sentence element is an adjective or adverb might be difficult at first. The important thing is determining what word the adjective or adverb modifies. If the words are not next to each other, it might be misplaced.

Misplaced Modifier:
An adjective or adverb may get separated from the word it modifies and describe the wrong word. While the reader will probably understand the meaning, the misplaced modifier makes the sentence confusing.

Incorrect:	Many cats are killed by cars **roaming unleashed**. ("Roaming unleashed" should modify *cats*, not *cars*.)
Correct:	Many cats roaming unleashed are killed by cars.

Incorrect:	The hospital did not disclose the man's name who committed suicide **at the request of the family**. ("At the request of the family" should modify *hospital*, not *suicide*.)
Correct:	The hospital, at the request of the family, did not disclose the man's name who committed suicide.

Incorrect:	Tom prepared a report on the benefits of overtime **for the personnel department**. ("For the personnel department" should modify *report*, not *overtime*.)
Correct:	Tom prepared a report for the personnel department on the benefits of overtime.

Incorrect:	My children selected a lunch from the menu **that was mostly sugar**. ("That was mostly sugar" should modify *lunch*, not *menu*.)
Correct:	My children selected a lunch that was mostly sugar from the menu.

Unclear:	The team **only** found the crucial evidence during the last search. (Does *only* refer to the evidence or the search?)
Clear:	The team found only the crucial evidence during the last search. (*Only* refers to the evidence.)
Clear:	The team found the crucial evidence only during the last search. (*Only* refers to the search.)

Dangling Modifier:
The dangling modifier, a common misplaced modifier, is an initial verbal phrase that does not describe the following element. Fix a dangling modifier by rewriting the dangling modifier as a dependent clause or by changing the following clause to start with what the dangling modifier describes.

Incorrect:	**Walking by the store**, a puppy caught my eye. (Who or what is walking by the store? "Walking by the store" modifies *puppy* and not the actual subject.)
Correct:	When I walked by the store, a puppy caught my eye.
Correct:	Walking by the store, I saw a puppy.

Incorrect:	**Reviewing the comments**, it was clear drastic changes are needed. ("Reviewing the comments" modifies *it* and not the actual subject.)
Correct:	After Amanda reviewed the comments, it was clear drastic changes are needed.
Correct:	Reviewing the comments, Amanda decided drastic changes are needed.

Incorrect:	**Driving to work**, my cellphone went dead. ("Driving to work" modifies *my cellphone* and not the actual subject.)
Correct:	While I was driving to work, my cellphone went dead.
Correct:	Driving to work, I noticed my cellphone went dead.

Incorrect:	**To get the free e-book**, the coupon code must be included. ("To get the free e-book" modifies *coupon code* and not the actual subject.)
Correct:	If you want to get the free e-book, the coupon code must be included.
Correct:	To get the free e-book, you must include the coupon code.

Incorrect:	**To understand the causes**, cancer is studied. ("To understand the causes" modifies *cancer* and not the actual subject.)
Correct:	Because researchers want to understand the causes, cancer is studied.
Correct:	To understand the causes, researchers study cancer.

Incorrect:	**After finishing the research**, the term paper was easy to write. ("After finishing the research" modifies *term paper* and not the actual subject.)
Correct:	After the student finished the research, the term paper was easy to write.
Correct:	After finishing the research, the student easily wrote the term paper.

Incorrect:	**By installing a thermostat**, the substantial cooling cost was reduced. ("By installing a thermostat" modifies *cooling cost* and not the actual subject.)
Correct:	When our client installed a thermostat, the substantial cooling cost was reduced.
Correct:	By installing a thermostat, our client reduced the substantial cooling cost.

Incorrect:	**Frequently used in colonial America**, historians agree shaming was an effective punishment. ("Frequently used in colonial America" should modify *shaming*, not *historians*.)
Correct:	Frequently used in colonial America, shaming was an effective punishment according to historians.

Pronoun Reference:

A pronoun (he, she, it, they) must clearly refer to the original noun. An unclear pronoun reference happens when the pronoun refers to more than one noun or when the pronoun is far removed from the noun and is a misplaced modifier.

Unclear:	Rebecca is often mistaken for Ashley, but **she** does not mind. (*She* might refer to either Rebecca or Ashley)
Clear:	Rebecca is often mistaken for Ashley, but Rebecca does not mind.
Clear:	Rebecca does not mind being mistaken for Ashley.

Unclear:	Jackson told Andrew that **he** was next on the overtime list. (*He* may refer to either Jackson or Andrew)
Clear:	Jackson said he is next on the overtime list.
Clear:	Jackson said Andrew is next on the overtime list.

<table>
<tr><td>Unclear:</td><td>Jacob found the bike in the basement his father used.
("his father used" should refer to bike, not basement)</td></tr>
<tr><td>Clear:</td><td>Jacob found the bike his father used in the basement.</td></tr>
</table>

<table>
<tr><td>Unclear:</td><td>While cleaning the backyard, I discovered an old wagon behind the shed my brother used.
("my brother used" should refers to wagon, not shed.)</td></tr>
<tr><td>Clear:</td><td>While cleaning the backyard, I discovered an old wagon my brother used behind the shed.</td></tr>
</table>

Use Better Verbs:

Verbs show action and are rightfully called the "heart of the sentence." They are either "strong" or "weak." The verbs *is, made, seem,* and *could* are weak verbs because they stall the sentence instead of moving it forward with action. To improve verb quality, do the following:

- Use a concrete verb.
- Avoid a verb with an *-ly* adverb (walked slowly).
- Avoid *it is, it was, there is*, and *there are*.
- Avoid *is, are, was,* and *were*.
- Avoid a verb with an *-ing* verb (started walking).
- Use active voice.

Use a Concrete Verb:

A vague verb (she ran) is less descriptive than a concrete verb (she sprinted). Substitute vague verbs with concrete verbs to provide the reader with a vivid mental image.

Vague Verb	Concrete Verb Substitutes
walk	stroll, march, glide, strut
run	race, rush, dart, dash, sprint
say	chat, rant, swear, banter, drone
sit	lounge, relax, recline, rest
made	design, form, assemble, invent

Use a thesaurus to find a substitute for a vague verb. However, replace a vague verb with only a commonly used verb, not an infrequently used verb. For example, a thesaurus lists *tramp* and *perambulation* as possible substitutes for *walk*. *Tramp* is a commonly used verb and might be an appropriate substitute based on the context. *Perambulation*, however, is a rarely used verb and is probably not an appropriate substitute.

Original:	Jack **sat** on the couch watching hockey. (The vague verb s*at* could be replaced.)
Revised:	Jack chilled on the couch watching hockey.

Original:	Rose **walked** to her car. (The vague verb *walked* could be replaced.)
Incorrect:	Rose ambulated to her car. (*Ambulated* is an infrequently used verb.)
Correct:	Rose strolled to her car.

Avoid a Verb With an -ly Adverb:
A vague verb can be bolstered with an *-ly* adverb (ran quickly, walked slowly). Replace the vague verb and *-ly* adverb with a concrete verb. The *-ly* adverb is sometimes redundant, so delete it.

Original:	The cat **ran quickly** through the room.
Revised:	The cat bolted through the room.

Original:	Tina **secretly listened** to her co-worker's vacation plans.
Revised:	Tina eavesdropped on her co-worker's vacation plans.

Original:	We **walked strenuously** through the snow.
Revised:	We trudged through the snow.

Original:	Thomas **turned quickly** around at the noise.
Revised:	Thomas turned around at the noise.
Revised:	Thomas spun around at the noise.

Avoid It Is, It Was, There Is, *and* There Are*:*
The purpose of starting a sentence with *it is, it was, there is,* or *there are* is to emphasize the subject. Often it only weakens the "real" verb and adds unnecessary words. Rewrite by beginning with the subject, and the sentence will gain clarity and conciseness.

Original:	**It was** clear drastic changes are necessary after reviewing the comments.
Revised:	Drastic changes are clearly necessary after reviewing the comments.

Original:	**There is** nothing wrong with the shipping costs.
Revised:	Nothing is wrong with the shipping costs.

Original:	**There are** three types of people who attend investment seminars.
Revised:	Three types of people attend investment seminars.

Avoid Is, Are, Was, *and* Were:
Weak verbs include forms of *to be* (is, are, was, were). These verbs only link parts of the sentence together and do not move it forward with action. Rewrite with a concrete verb, if possible.

Original:	What Sarah wanted **was** a red Ford Mustang.
Revised:	Sarah wanted a red Ford Mustang.

Original:	The focus of the training **is** first aid.
Revised:	The training focuses on first aid.

Original:	Robert's email **is** a summary of the new laws.
Revised:	Robert's email summarizes the new laws.

Original:	The house **is** old and **is** in danger of collapsing during a strong earthquake.
Revised:	The old house could collapse during a strong earthquake.

Avoid a Verb With an -ing Verb:
Consider the following original sentence and rewrite:

Original:	The worried mother **began pacing** back and forth.
Revised:	The worried mother paced back and forth.

In the original sentence, *began* only weakens *pacing*, so delete it. Consider deleting the verbs *started, began, is, was,* and *were* with an *-ing* verb.

Original:	Loren **began jogging** on the trail.
Revised:	Loren jogs on the trail.
Revised	Loren jogged on the trail.

Original:	He **started yelling** for help.
Revised:	He yells for help.
Revised:	He yelled for help.

Original:	Rose **is walking** to her car.
Revised:	Rose walks to her car.

Original:	A mob **was starting** to form.
Revised:	A mob started to form.
Revised:	A mob formed.

Use Active Voice:
The Chicago Manual of Style (Section 5.118) states:

> Voice shows whether the subject acts (active voice) or is acted upon (passive voice)—that is, whether the subject performs or receives the action of the verb. . . .

> As a matter of style, passive voice is typically, though not always, inferior to active voice. The choice between active and passive voice may depend on which point of view is desired.

An author constructs the passive voice by combining the verb *to be* (is, was, were) with the desired verb's past participle (built, stole, filled): is built, was stolen, were filled.

Use passive voice when the object needs emphasis or when the subject is unknown or not important. If passive voice is not used for one of these reasons, active voice is preferred.

- My car was stolen by masked thieves.
  - The object (my car) needed emphasis.

- A complaint was filed against Jim.
  - Who filed the complaint is unknown.

- The house was built in 1995.
  - Who built the house is unknown or not important.

To rewrite passive voice, find and begin with the subject. In many passive voice sentences, *by* precedes the subject.

Original:	He **was hit** by the baseball.
Revised:	The baseball hit him.

Original:	My car **was stolen** by masked thieves.
Revised:	Masked thieves stole my car.

Original:	The data transmission **was accomplished** by the new system.
Revised:	The new system accomplished the data transmission.
Revised:	The new system transmitted the data.

Original:	The play **was canceled** by the committee.
Revised:	The committee canceled the play.

Original:	Many cats roaming unleashed **are killed** by cars.
Revised:	Cars kill many cats roaming unleashed.

Original:	The new law **is seen** by most businesses as unfair.
Revised:	Most businesses see the new law as unfair.

<u>Use Parallelism</u>:
Parallelism improves clarity through grammatical consistency. Parallelism means words or phrases with the same function must have the same grammatical form. Coordinating conjunctions (and, or) signal words or phrases with the same function.

Not Parallel:	The exercise proved to be **a challenge** and **stimulating**. (The noun *challenge* is not parallel with the adjective *stimulating*.)
Parallel:	The exercise proved to be challenging and stimulating.
Parallel:	The exercise proved to be a challenge and a stimulant.

Not Parallel:	The company **is using** new advertising techniques and **produces** more sales. (The verb phrases have different forms.)
Parallel:	The company uses new advertising techniques and produces more sales.
Parallel:	The company is using new advertising techniques and is producing more sales.

Not Parallel:	The CEO refused either option—**to sell** at a loss or **donate** the property. (*Either* signals needed parallelism.)
Parallel:	The CEO refused either option—to sell at a loss or to donate the property.

Not Parallel:	Pam entered the room **quietly**; Tom with **recklessness**. (The adverb and adjective are not parallel.)
Parallel:	Pam entered the room quietly; Tom, recklessly.

Not Parallel:	Did you see the mama **bear**, papa **bear**, and the **young cub**? (*Young cub* not parallel with *bear* phrasing.)
Parallel:	Did you see the mama bear, papa bear, and baby bear?

For a series of parallel prepositional phrases, repeat the preposition unless each phrase begins with the same preposition.

Not Parallel:	I searched for the missing sock **in** the sock drawer, the laundry hamper, and **under** the bed. (The prepositional phrases do not begin with the same preposition. Therefore, repeat the preposition.)
Parallel:	I searched for the missing sock **in** the sock drawer, **in** the laundry hamper, and **under** the bed.
Parallel: **(Edited)**	I searched for the missing sock **in** the sock drawer, the laundry hamper, and the bedroom. (Because all prepositional phrases begin with *in*, do not repeated it.)

<u>Sentence Length and Type</u>:
The longer the sentence, the worse the comprehension rate. After a sentence contains more than seventeen words, the comprehension rate drops at approximately 3 percent per word.

Sentence Length (Words)	Comprehension Rate (%)
14	90
17	85
20	75
28	50
37	25
43	10

Source: Ann Wylie, "How to Make Your Copy More Readable," 2009.

Martin Cutts, author of *Oxford Guide to Plain English*, offers the following advice: "Over the whole document, make the average sentence length 15–20 words." Martin's recommendation results in an average comprehension rate of 75 to 90 percent.

Many word processors and internet websites can provide the average sentence length. In Microsoft Word, the average sentence length is located under "Readability Statistics." The website *slickwrite.com* provides a wide range of information about your document: average sentence length, readability index, types of sentences used, and so on.

When the document's average sentence length is too high, what can an author do to reduce it? First, edit sentences for clarity and conciseness. This should result in shorter sentences and may solve the problem.

Second, scan the document and look for very long sentences that exceed 25 words. Do not count words; just eyeball it. Simple, compound, and complex sentences are normally under 25 words. Very long sentences are typically compound-complex sentences, so break a portion of them into two sentences.

Vary Sentence Length:
Readers like variety. Do not write all short sentences to guarantee excellent comprehension. Instead, vary the sentence length from about 8 to 28 words, but keep the average sentence length between 15 and 20 words.

Vary Sentence Type:
Again, readers like variety. Authors frequently write only one or two sentence types. The lack of variety is acceptable for the first draft. During intense sentence-level editing, rewrite sentences to provide a mix of simple, compound, complex, and compound-complex sentences. Rewriting techniques include:

- Combining two simple sentences into a compound sentence.
- Combining two simple sentences into a complex sentence using a subordinating conjunction.
- Breaking a compound sentence into simple sentences.
- Rewriting a compound sentence as a complex sentence.
- Combining sentences into a compound-complex sentence.
- Breaking a compound-complex sentence into two sentences.

A cliché is a frequently used phrase (*from the frying pan to the fire* or *reinvent the wheel*). Readers like fresh and original, and clichés are neither fresh nor original. Authors should avoid and rewrite a cliché whenever possible.

Common Clichés:

acid test	in a nutshell
back to the drawing board	in the nick of time
beauty is only skin deep	in the same boat
beyond the shadow of doubt	ladder of success
blind as a bat	light as a feather
bright and early	moving experience
burn the midnight oil	needle in a haystack
busy as a bee/beaver	open-and-shut case
butterflies in the stomach	out of the corner of the eye
cool as a cucumber	pain in the butt
cool, calm, and collected	pretty as a picture
crack of dawn	rat race
crystal clear	rude awakening
dead as a doornail	sad but true
dog-eat-dog world	sick as a dog
don't hold your breath	sigh of relief
easier said than done	slow as molasses
easy as pie	spread like wildfire
every cloud has a silver lining	stick out like a sore thumb
face the music	strong as an ox
fall between the cracks	to all intents and purposes
flat as a pancake	to be fair/honest
first and foremost	to make a long story short
forever and a day	trial and error
gentle as a lamb	when it rains, it pours
head over heels	when push comes to shove
hit the nail on the head	white as a sheet
hour of need	worth its weight in gold

Conciseness:

> A sentence should contain no unnecessary words, a paragraph no unnecessary sentences, for the same reason that a drawing should have no unnecessary lines and a machine no unnecessary parts. This requires not that the writer make all his sentences short, or that he avoid all detail and treat his subjects only in outline, but that every word tell.
> —William Strunk Jr., *The Elements of Style*

Conciseness declutters sentences by removing unnecessary words that obscure meaning and reduce comprehension. **Make every word count**, and whenever possible, write a sentence in fewer words.

To achieve conciseness

- use better verbs (see page 22).
- use active voice (see page 25).
- remove unnecessary words and phrases.

<u>Remove Unnecessary Words and Phrases:</u>

Shorten Phrases:
A phrase might include a few unnecessary words, or possibly it could be replaced with a single word. Appendix B (List 1) lists phrases that may be shortened.

<u>**Original**</u>	<u>**Revised**</u>
a large number of	many, much
a lot of	many
a small number of	some
at all times	always
at this point in time	now
in cases that	if, when
in regards to	about, on
on a regular basis	regularly
until such time as	until
with reference to the fact that	about, concerning

Nearly one-third of Appendix B (List 1) entries contain the word *of*, so let it be a signal word for possible revision. Two common patterns include the following:

a _______ of
the _______ of

Original	**Revised**
a lot of	many
a small number of	some
the majority of	many, most

Cut Parenthetical Expressions and Empty Words:
Removing a parenthetical expression will not affect the meaning of a sentence (Appendix A, Section 7-1). Therefore, delete most parenthetical expressions.

Parenthetical Expressions:

Original	**Revised**
clearly	(remove)
for your information	(remove)
generally	(remove)
in fact	(remove)
in my opinion	(remove)
needless to say	(remove)
of course	(remove)
obviously	(remove)
unfortunately	(remove)

Delete or revise an "empty word" and any accompanying words. Empty words include:

area	element	kind	quality
aspect	factor	level	situation
case	field	manner	thing
character	instance	nature	type

The intensifiers *extremely, quite, really, severely,* and **very** are often empty words that may be deleted.

Appendix B (List 2) lists parenthetical expressions and empty word phrases that may be deleted or revised.

Original	**Revised**
by their nature	(delete)
last but not lest	(delete)
more or less	(delete)
on the whole	(delete)
that	(possible deletion)
the (empty word) of	(possible deletion)
the fact that	(delete)

The phrase *the fact that* occurs in many empty word phrases, and the words may be deleted. For example, the phrase *due to the fact that* may be replaced with *because*, and the phrase *despite the fact that* may be shortened to *despite*.

An author is not required to shorten every long phrase or to remove all parenthetical expressions and empty word phrases. **Editing exceptions include the need for emphasis, parallelism, and word variety.**

Shorten Verb Phrases:
Scrutinize the verb. Some verb phrases may be replaced with a shorter verb phrase or even a single verb. Appendix B (List 3) lists verb phrases that may be revised. The following example replaces four words with one word:

- Jan **has the ability to** run an eight-minute mile.
- Jan **can** run an eight-minute mile.

The following five verbs signal a verb phrase that might be revised or shortened:

arrive
make
place
put
take

Original:	Aaron had to **make** a stop at the bank.
Revised:	Aaron had to stop at the bank.
Revised:	Aaron stopped at the bank.

| **Original:** | The attorneys **arrived** at a compromise after a private, two-hour discussion. |
| **Revised:** | The attorneys compromised after a private, two-hour discussion. |

| **Original:** | My manager promised to **take** a look into the matter. |
| **Revised:** | My manager promised to look into the matter. |

| **Original:** | I **would have been able to** attend the meeting, but a car accident delayed me. |
| **Revised:** | I could have attended the meeting, but a car accident delayed me. |

| **Original:** | The professor **gave** a lecture at the library. |
| **Revised:** | The professor lectured at the library. |

Proper Use the Past Perfect Tense:
Both the simple past tense (ate, called) and the past perfect tense (had eaten, had called) describe an action in the past. Use the past perfect tense when one past action happens before another past action.

- Jeff had eaten dinner before Kimberly called.

The sentence describes two past actions: Jeff ate and Kimberly called. Jeff ate before Kimberly called. Therefore, use the past perfect with Jeff's action (had eaten), and use the simple past with Kimberly's action (called).

A sentence usually falls into the "past perfect" editing category when the context only describes a single past action but uses the past perfect tense. Assume no other past action in the context for the following example:

- My company had spent the funds unwisely.

The sentence describes only one past action, so the past perfect tense is not required. Instead, use the simple past tense.

- My company spent the funds unwisely.

Possible Past Perfect Revisions:

Original	**Revised**
had (past perfect)	(simple past)
had been	was
had begun	began
had done	done
had gone	went
had made	made

Original:	The new alarm **had gone** off accidentally.
Revised:	The new alarm went off accidentally.

Original:	I **had** just **seen** Kathy on Tuesday.
Revised:	I just saw Kathy on Tuesday.

Original:	Phil **had made** some barbecued ribs.
Revised:	Phil made some barbecued ribs.
Revised:	Phil barbecued some ribs.

Rewrite Zombie Nouns:
Rewrite a "zombie noun" or a noun created by adding the suffix *-tion, -sion, -ance, -ence, -ment, -ity,* or *-ism* to a verb or adjective. Zombie nouns often need additional words, especially prepositions.

Verb/Adjective	**Zombie Noun**
decide	decision
interfere	interference
argue	argument
intense	intensity

Zombie nouns are more common in legal, academic, and bureaucratic writing. Appendix B (List 4) lists zombie nouns that may be revised.

| **Original:** | The **determination of** the court was not guilty. |
| **Revised:** | The court decided not guilty. |

| **Original:** | During the **presentation of** the department's budget, the CFO visited. |
| **Revised:** | While Reta presented the department's budget, the CFO visited. |

| **Original:** | Andrew is in **possession of** the latest computer equipment for online gaming. |
| **Revised:** | Andrew possesses the latest computer equipment for online gaming. |

A *-tion* or *-sion* zombie noun followed by an *of* phrase may be rewritten using an *-ing* verb.

Original	**Revised**
creation of the plan	creating the plan
discussion of the situation	discussing the situation
addition of the requirement	adding the requirement

Shorten a Relative Clause:
Sometimes, the subject (that, which, who) and verb in a relative clause may be deleted.

| **Original:** | Those **who are** invited to participate should arrive one hour early. |
| **Revised:** | Those invited to participate should arrive one hour early. |

| **Original:** | The result is a product **that is** geared to the consumer. |
| **Revised:** | The result is a product geared to the consumer. |

Original:	There is only one open seat **that exists** on the committee.
Revised:	There is only one open seat on the committee.
Revised:	One open seat exists on the committee.

Remove Unnecessary Repetition:
While repeating a keyword for emphasis will improve clarity or comprehension, repeated words normally weaken the writing because readers value variety. Always avoid starting nearby sentences with the same word.

Unnecessary repetition includes double nouns, double adjectives, and double adverbs.

Original	**Revised**
green in color	green
square in shape	square
flawless perfection	perfection
general consensus	consensus
proven fact	fact
one and only	only
rules and regulations	rules, regulations
fair and equitable	fair, equitable

Appendix B (List 5) lists examples of unnecessary repetition that may be revised.

Original:	Pat referred to the **basic and fundamental** principles of physics.
Revised:	Pat referred to the fundamental principles of physics.

Original:	I paid **a total of $600** for the new prescription glasses.
Revised:	I paid $600 for the new prescription glasses.

Original:	The **plain and simple** truth is UFOs exist.
Revised:	The simple truth is UFOs exist.

Original:	The **original creator** of the World Wide Web is Sir Timothy Berners-Lee.
Revised:	The creator of the World Wide Web is Sir Timothy Berners-Lee.

<u>Rewrite Prepositional Phrases</u>:
Do not overuse prepositional phrases. *The Chicago Manual of Style* recommends one preposition for every ten to fifteen words. If the average sentence length is fifteen to twenty words (see page 29), a sentence should have only one or two prepositions, maybe three in a long sentence.

Remove an Unnecessary Prepositional Phrase:
Remove a prepositional phrase if the context provides the information. In the following two examples, the author is writing about a report or book. Therefore, the prepositional phrases in boldface are not required because the information is redundant due to the context.

Original:	The most useful section **in the report** is the historical background.
Revised:	The most useful section is the historical background.

Original:	The second chapter **of the book** covered consumer debt.
Revised:	The second chapter covered consumer debt.

Rewrite with a Better Verb:
Replace a prepositional phrase with a better verb (see page 22).

Original:	The building **shook with great force**.
Revised:	The building trembled.

Original:	The proposal was **under review** by the manager.
Revised:	The proposal was examined by the manager.
Revised:	The manager examined the proposal.

Original:	Emergency preparedness can **make up for** panic buying.
Revised:	Emergency preparedness can prevent panic buying.

Rewrite to Active Voice:
Remove a prepositional phrase by rewriting the sentence in active voice (see page 25).

Original:	My car **was stolen by** my brother
Revised:	My brother stole my car.

Original:	He **was hit by** the baseball.
Revised:	The baseball hit him.

Rewrite Zombie Nouns:
Rewrite zombie nouns that often require additional words, especially prepositions (see page 35).

Original:	The **determination of** the court was not guilty.
Revised:	The court decided not guilty.

Rewrite as an Adjective or Adverb:
Rewrite a prepositional phrase as an adjective or adverb.

Adjective:

Original:	The **licensing for my vehicle** should be completed this week.
Revised:	My vehicle licensing should be completed this week.

Original:	The **goal of the marketing** is to increase sales.
Revised:	The marketing goal is to increase sales.

Original:	The **proposal for acquisition** is under review.
Revised:	The acquisition proposal is under review.

Original:	The **chair of the committee** voted against the **application for variance**.
Revised:	The committee chair voted against the variance application.

Adverb:

Original:	The Atlantic storm struck **with force**.
Revised:	The Atlantic storm struck forcefully.

Original:	I accepted the large assignment **with hesitation**.
Revised:	I hesitantly accepted the large assignment.

Original:	My employer sent me **without delay**.
Revised:	My employer sent me immediately.

Original:	One factor **of extreme importance** is the **difference in age**.
Revised:	One extremely important factor is the age difference.

Rewrite as a Genitive:
Rewrite a prepositional phrase, especially an *of the* phrase, as a genitive.

Original:	The **house of my client** sits on a hill
Revised:	My client's house sits on a hill.

Original:	In the **opinion of the CEO**, additional marketing is unnecessary.
Revised:	In the CEO's opinion, additional marketing is unnecessary.

Original:	The **top managers of the company** thought the marketing plan would increase sales.
Revised:	The company's top managers thought the marketing plan would increase sales.

Original:	The **efficacy of the vaccine** is controversial.
Revised:	The vaccine's efficacy is controversial.

Original:	The **objective of the meeting** is to approve the budget.
Revised:	The meeting's objective is to approve the budget.

Sentence-Level Polish

After rewriting sentences for clarity and conciseness, edit sentences focusing on correctness. Also, verify every sentence is one of the four sentence types, reworking it as needed. Some sentences may need rewriting for clarity and conciseness. Most editing, however, will address grammar, spelling, capitalization, number formatting, abbreviation, punctuation, and so on.

Because a self-editor is more likely to read over errors, they should (see page 18):

- Allow time between editing passes.
- Read slowly.
- Change the font size.
- Take breaks while editing.

Four Sentence Types:
Confirm each sentence is either a simple, compound, complex, or compound-complex. Analyzing the structure of each clause, phrase, and sentence element will help find grammar errors and will determine the correct punctuation.

Correctness:
What is correct grammar, spelling, capitalization, number formatting, and punctuation? Correctness means the document follows the rules of a style guide like the *Chicago Manual of Style* or *The Gregg Reference Manual*. Popular style guides include:

- ***The Associated Press Stylebook*** (AP) for newspapers and magazines.

- ***The Chicago Manual of Style*** (CMOS) for books.

- ***The Gregg Reference Manual*** (GRM) for business.

- ***Modern Language Association Handbook*** (MLA) for academic writing, especially in the humanities.

- ***Publication Manual for the American Psychological Association*** (APA) for academic writing, especially in the social sciences.

Many rules in the popular style guides are the same or similar. They agree on about 90 percent of the rules for punctuation, and they agree on about 75 precent of the rules for capitalization, abbreviation usage, and number formatting. While each style guide has its own way of documenting sources, there are many similarities.

Grammar:
Many people cringe when they hear the word *grammar*. The good news is some grammar topics were already covered—the four sentence types, dangling and misplaced modifiers, parallel construction, and use of the past perfect tense. Here are several more topics.

Subject-Verb Agreement:
The subject and verb must agree. A singular subject uses a singular verb, and a plural subject uses a plural verb.

Incorrect:	The girl sing.
Correct:	The girl sings. (or: The girls sing.)
Incorrect:	The boys plays.
Correct:	The boys play (or: The boy plays.)

The above errors are usually unintentional and easily corrected during editing. Certain situations are more problematic (see following sections). To avoid a subject-verb agreement error, determine the subject for each verb and check if they agree.

Indefinite Pronouns. An indefinite pronoun does not refer to a specific person or thing. Most indefinite pronouns use a singular verb, and a few use a plural verb. Some use a singular or plural verb depending if the subject is singular or plural.

Singular	anybody, anyone, anything, each, either, every, everybody, everyone, everything, much, neither, nobody, no one, nothing, one, somebody, someone, something.
Plural	both, few, many, others, several
Singular or Plural	all, any, more, most, none, some

A "singular" indefinite pronoun always refers to a singular person or thing. A "plural" indefinite pronoun always refers to a plural person or thing.

- **Something** <u>is</u> not right about the new law.
- **Everyone** <u>sees</u> the problem.
- **Few** do not <u>see</u> the problem, though.
- **Many** <u>are</u> working on a solution.

A "singular or plural" indefinite pronoun may refer to either a singular or plural person or thing, and it often occurs with an *of* phrase. Use a singular verb when the indefinite pronoun refers to a singular subject, and use a plural verb when it refers to a plural subject.

- Is funding available? Yes, **some** <u>is</u> available.
  - *Some* refers to *funding* in the previous sentence.
- **Some** of the people <u>are</u> obnoxious.
  - *Some* refers to *people*.

Subjects Joined by "And." Two or more subjects joined by *and* require a plural verb.

- **Rebecca and Susan** <u>are</u> traveling together.
- **Steve and Ken** <u>are</u> brothers.

Exceptions to the above rule include when the subject or subject parts are preceded by the words *each* or *every*, refer to the same person or thing, or form a single idea.

- <u>Each</u> **man and woman** <u>is</u> protected by the same rights.
- The union's **president and treasurer** <u>is</u> Janet Smith.
- **Peanut butter and jelly** <u>is</u> my favorite sandwich.

Subjects Joined by "Or." When *or* joins two subjects, the verb agrees with the subject nearest the verb. To avoid awkwardness, place the plural subject next to the verb when one subject is singular and the other subject is plural.

- Either the accountant or the **banker** <u>knows</u> the cost.
- Do those dressers or **cabinets** <u>have</u> adequate storage?
- Did the boss or the **workers** <u>find</u> the reason?

Collective Nouns. A collective noun refers to a group of people (committee, family, team), animals (flock, herd, pack), or things (collection, set).

When all members of a collective noun act together as a group, which is the usual situation, use a singular verb.

- The **orchestra** often <u>plays</u> at the Civic Centre.
- My **family** <u>is</u> united against injustice.

When members of a collective noun act separately as individuals, use a plural verb.

- The **orchestra** <u>are</u> tuning their instruments.
- My **family** <u>have</u> now gone in different directions.

Because a collective noun with a plural verb may sound awkward, consider adding the word *members* to the sentence.

- The orchestra **members** <u>are</u> tuning their instruments.
- My family **members** <u>have</u> gone in different directions.

Subject is a Phrase or Clause. When the subject of a sentence is a phrase or clause, use a singular verb.

- **Reading this book** <u>is</u> an excellent way to improve your English writing.
- **The junk mail I receive daily** <u>goes</u> straight into the recycle bin.

Words Between Subject and Verb. Ignore any words between the subject and the verb when evaluating the subject-verb agreement. A typical problem occurs when a noun of an intervening prepositional phrase immediately precedes the verb and the intervening noun of the propositional phrase has a different number than the subject.

- The **car** with the new *tires* <u>drives</u> wonderfully.
- Several **things** with the new *operating system* <u>are</u> causing an error.
- The **reaction** inside the large storage *tanks* <u>stops</u> because of chemical bonding.

Consistent Person, Number, and Tense:
In grammar, *person* refers to first person (I, we), second person (you), or third person (he, she, it, they); *number* refers singular or plural; and *tense* refers to a verb's time (past, present, future).

Be Consistent in Person. Inconsistency usually occurs when referring to people with both the second and third person or with both the second person and a generic noun. (See page 49 for the use of the phrase *he or she*.)

Incorrect:	If a <u>person</u> is late, <u>you</u> may be fired.
Correct:	If a <u>person</u> is late, <u>he or she</u> may be fired.
Correct:	If <u>you</u> are late, <u>you</u> may be fired.

Incorrect:	<u>Plumbers</u> are taught <u>you</u> can learn to fix pipes with practice.
Correct:	<u>Plumbers</u> are taught <u>they</u> can learn to fix pipes with practice.

Be Consistent in Number. Inconsistency usually occurs between a noun and a pronoun (see page 22).

Incorrect:	If a <u>person</u> is late, <u>they</u> should be fired.
Correct:	If a <u>person</u> is late, <u>he or she</u> should be fired.
Correct:	If <u>people</u> are late, <u>they</u> should be fired.

Incorrect:	A <u>plumber</u> fixes pipes; <u>they</u> do not fix outlets.
Correct:	<u>Plumbers</u> fix pipes; <u>they</u> do not fix outlets.

Be Consistent in Tense. Inconsistency usually occurs when unnecessarily changing between the past and present tense.

Incorrect:	Maria <u>walked</u> in late, and she <u>paces</u> around the office before sitting down.
Correct:	Maria <u>walked</u> in late, and she <u>paced</u> around the office before sitting down.

Incorrect:	Tom <u>crashed</u> the car, but somehow he <u>pulls</u> out his cellphone and <u>calls</u> 911.
Correct:	Tom <u>crashed</u> the car, but somehow he <u>pulled</u> out his cellphone and <u>called</u> 911.

That vs. Which:
The pronouns *that, which*, and *who* introduce a relative clause, and using *that* or *which* depends on the type of relative clause. An essential relative clause defines or restricts the meaning of the element it modifies. A nonessential relative clause only adds information and could be removed without affecting the meaning of the sentence (Appendix A, Section 10 and 11).

Use *who* to refer to people and named pets.

- **Mary** is the manager <u>who</u> manages accident claims.
- The vet examined **Bell** <u>who</u> was not eating or drinking.

Use *that* to refer to a collective noun consisting of people or to introduce an essential clause referring to a place, object, or animal.

- The **team** <u>that</u> wins the championship receives a $5,000 prize.
- Where are the **keys** <u>that</u> I left on the desk?
- **Computers** <u>that</u> are used for gaming are expensive.

Use *which* to introduce a nonessential clause referring to a place, object, or animal. *Which* <u>may</u> be used for an essential relative clause when *that* has been already used in the sentence. A nonessential relative clause is set off with commas (see page 58).

- My **truck,** <u>which</u> is a Ford F-150, needs an oil change.
- October's expense **report**, <u>which</u> was emailed Friday, contained a blatant error.
- Management must enforce the **rules** <u>that</u> they made recently <u>that</u> were controversial.
  - or "which were controversial."
  - The sentence is best written: Management must enforce the recent, controversial rules.

The GRM and *The Little, Brown Handbook* (2016) state some writers now use *which* to introduce both essential and nonessential clauses. However, CMOS, MLA, and AP use *that* for an essential clause and *which* for a nonessential clause.

Contraction Usage:
Common contractions include the following:

aren't	don't	I've	that's	who's
can't	he's	it's	they'll	won't
couldn't	I'd	let's	they're	you'll
didn't	I'll	she's	wasn't	you're
doesn't	I'm	shouldn't	what's	you've

The popular style guides agree contractions should <u>not</u> be used in formal writing. Formal writing includes academic writing, a newspaper or magazine article, a book, a business letter or report, or an email to an unfamiliar co-worker. The widely used contraction *o'clock* is permitted in formal writing.

Contractions are permitted in informal writing, but style guides advise not to overuse them. Informal writing includes a Facebook or Twitter post, a letter to a friend or family member, or an email to a familiar co-worker.

Gender Bias:
Generic nouns like *customer, doctor, employee, manager, parent,* and *supervisor* can refer to any gender. When a generic noun is singular and has a known gender based on context, use the appropriate singular pronoun.

- My **doctor** immediately responds to <u>her</u> emails.
    - The doctor is known to be female.

- My friend's **manager** failed to perform <u>his</u> duties.
    - The manager is known to be male.

Gender bias might occur when a pronoun refers to a generic noun with an unknown gender because the pronoun must apply to all genders. In the past, authors used the pronoun *he*. The pronoun *she* occurred with female-dominated professions like *secretary, teacher,* and *nurse*. Today, using *he, she, his,* or *her* with a generic noun is no longer acceptable in formal or informal writing.

Some style guides allow the occasional use of the phrases "he or she" or "his or her" with a generic noun. This is no longer necessary with the recent endorsement of singular *they* (see Number 5 below). Do not use *he/she, his/her, him/her,* or *s/he*.

The following methods may remove gender bias, and context determines when a method is applicable. Rewrite the sentence if gender bias cannot be removed.

1. *Omit the Pronoun.* Sometimes the pronoun is not needed.

Original:	The **doctor** never responds to <u>his</u> emails.
Revised:	The **doctor** never responds to emails.

2. *Replace the Pronoun with an Article (a* or *the).*

Original:	The **manager** forgot to open <u>her</u> package.
Revised:	The **manager** forgot to open <u>the</u> package.

3. *Repeat the Noun.* This method works best when the noun and pronoun are separated by many words.

Original:	A **parent** should be careful not to criticize a child because <u>her</u> words may have long-lasting effects.
Revised:	A **parent** should be careful not to criticize a child because a <u>parent's</u> words may have long-lasting effects.

4. *Change the Noun to a Plural.* This method removes the gender bias, but it may change the meaning of the sentence.

Original:	A **politician** should always conduct <u>himself</u> appropriately.
Revised:	**Politicians** should always conduct <u>themselves</u> appropriately.

5. *Use the Pronoun "They."* The term "Singular They" means using the plural pronoun *they* to refer to a singular generic noun. For many years, Singular They has been used in informal writing while its acceptance in formal writing steadily grew.

Both CMOS (2017 print) and AP (2019 print) state Singular They in formal writing is acceptable but should be avoided. Both recommend rewording first.

Starting in 2019, Singular They gained significant acceptance in formal writing. First, the *Merriam-Webster.com Dictionary* added Singular They as a definition entry in September 2019. Second, the APA and the Modern Language Association website (publisher of the *MLA Handbook*) endorsed its use in 2020.

Original:	A **teacher** should not discipline a student because <u>her</u> actions may fall outside the school's policy.
Revised:	A **teacher** should not discipline a student because <u>their</u> actions may fall outside the school's policy.

Original:	Every **taxpayer** must file <u>his or her</u> tax return on or before April 15.
Revised:	Every **taxpayer** must file <u>their</u> tax return on or before April 15.

Some nouns reflect a gender bias and should be replaced with a generic or gender-neutral word.

<u>**Original**</u>	<u>**Revised**</u>
businessman	business person
chairman	chair, committee head
congressman	congressional representative
fireman	firefighter
mailman	mail carrier
man-made	machine-made, manufactured, synthetic
manhole	maintenance hole
mankind	human beings, humanity, people
policeman/policewoman	police officer
steward/stewardess	flight attendant
workmen	workers

<u>Spelling</u>:
For spelling, three of the five popular style guides use ***Merriam-Webster's Collegiate Dictionary*** (MW Dictionary). It is an abridgment of the 450,000-word *Webster's Third New International Dictionary*. The latest edition of the MW Dictionary, the Eleventh Edition, was published in 2007 and contains about 225,000 words.

The MW Dictionary has a free online version, the *Merriam-Webster.com Dictionary*, available at *www.merriam-webster.com*. The online dictionary contains 240,000 words and is regularly updated.

The Associated Press Stylebook uses a different dictionary, the *Webster's New World College Dictionary* (NW Dictionary). The latest edition of the NW Dictionary, the Fifth Edition, was published in 2014 (updated 2016, 2018, and 2020) and contains about 165,000 words. NW Dictionary entries (2014 edition) are available online for free at *www.yourdictionary.com*.

<u>Style Guide</u>	**<u>Dictionary</u>**
American Psychological Association (APA)	*Merriam-Webster.com Dictionary*
The *Associated Press Stylebook* (AP)	*Webster's New World College Dictionary*
The *Chicago Manual of Style* (CMOS)	*Webster's Third New International Dictionary* (unabridged dictionary) or *Merriam-Webster's Collegiate Dictionary* (abridged dictionary)
The Gregg Reference Manual (GRM)	*Merriam-Webster's Collegiate Dictionary*
MLA Handbook (MLA)	No Preference (Eighth Ed. [2016] primarily followed *Merriam-Webster's Collegiate Dictionary*)

<u>Punctuation Overview</u>:

The more grammar a person knows, the better the punctuation will be. To punctuation well, a person must be able to

- identify independent and dependent clauses.
- identify verbal and prepositional phrases.
- identify coordinating and subordinating conjunctions.
- identify conjunctive adverbs and transitional expressions.
- determine if a sentence element is essential or nonessential.

The grammar reference in Appendix A covers these topics.

The Period:
A period separates thoughts, and it ends a sentence for a statement or command. English has four sentence types based on structure: simple, compound, complex, and compound-complex (see pages 8 to 11).

The Question Mark:
A question mark ends a sentence asking a direct question.

The Exclamation Mark:
An exclamation mark ends a sentence for a strong command or statement. It should be used sparingly.

The Comma:
A comma is a general separator. It is considered a neutral separator compared to the dash (emphasis) or parentheses (de-emphasis).

A comma separates:

- Equal sentence elements: coordinate adjectives, items in a series, and independent clauses separated with a coordinating conjunction.

- Unequal sentence elements: a direct quotation, a nonessential element, an introductory element, parts of a date or address, and so on.

When an item in a series or a nonessential element already contains a comma, use semicolons to separate the items in a series and a dash or parentheses to separate the nonessential element.

The Semicolon:
A semicolon could be considered a weak period or a strong comma. It predominantly separates equal sentence elements.

- Independent clauses separated without a coordinating conjunction.
- Independent clauses in a compound sentence that have internal commas where a misreading is likely.
- Items in a series containing internal commas.

The Colon:
A colon generally separates unequal sentence elements: an independent clause from a series, appositive, or explanation.

An independent clause always precedes a colon.

The Hyphen:
The hyphen has several uses. Primarily, it joins the words in a compound word (well-known), It also joins some prefixes and suffixes (ex-husband, pre-1990).

The Dash:
While both the en dash (–) and em dash (—) punctuate sentences, the em dash is commonly called a "dash."

Do not put a space on either side of an en dash or em dash. Use two connected hyphens (--) when the em dash character is not available, and use one hyphen when the en dash character is not available.

An em dash is used to
- separate a sudden shift in thought.
- separate an end-of-sentence afterthought.
- separate a nonessential element with internal commas.
- separate an introductory series from the main clause.
- substitute emphatically for a comma, colon, semicolon, or parentheses.

The en dash is mainly used to show a number range (137–142, 2013–2017).

Quotation Marks:
Double quotation marks enclose a direct quotation from a person or document. Single quotation marks enclose a direct quotation within a direct quotation.

Use quotation marks to enclose the title of a work within a larger work, like a book chapter or magazine article. (Italicize the title of a book, magazine, or newspaper.) Quotation marks are also used to emphasize a word or phrase.

Parentheses:
Use parentheses to separate a nonessential element containing internal commas or to separate an element not grammatically related to the sentence.

Brackets:
Use brackets to show changes or additions to a direct quotation or to show parentheses within parentheses.

The Apostrophe:
The apostrophe forms the possessive, shows the plural of a lowercase letter, shows the omission of letters or numbers, and creates some verb forms.

Punctuation Rule Numbering:
The punctuation rules are numbered and in boldface for better comprehension and reference.

<u>The Period</u>:

Rule 1. Statement or Command
Use a period to end a statement or command.

Statement:
- The suspect has an alibi.
- I do not drive above the speed limit.

Use a period after a grammatically incomplete statement that represents a complete simple sentence. Use an incomplete sentence intentionally, cautiously, and sparingly.
- Sandra lost her cellphone. **No Problem**.
- When the CEO decides, it is final. **Period**.

Command:
- Speak louder.
- Please drive faster.
- Drive faster, please.

Only separate the word *please* with a comma when it occurs at the end of a sentence.

<u>The Exclamation Mark</u>:

Rule 2. Strong Statement, Command, or Interjection
Use an exclamation mark after a strong statement, command, interjection, or rhetorical question. Use exclamation marks sparingly.

- Lives depend on us. We cannot make a mistake!
- A poisonous snake slivered behind a log. Be careful!
- Shit! I forgot to pack any clothes.
- Who calls to say "hello" at 3:30 a.m.!

An exclamation mark shouts at the reader. Therefore, there must be a significant amount of amazement, astonishment, disbelief, enthusiasm, skepticism, surprise, urgency, or other strong feeling. When the sentence does not have a strong feeling, use a period. Use a comma after a mild interjection.

- A garter snake slivered behind a bush. Be careful.
- Shoot, I forgot to pack my toothbrush.

<u>The Comma</u>:

Rule 3. Independent Clauses with Conjunction
Use a comma to separate two independent clauses joined with a coordinating conjunction.

- I went to the grocery store, and I saw a friend from high school.
- My investigation notes start on page 21, but my analysis of the accident's cause begins on page 53.
- I felt ill, and my friend left.

If the independent clauses are very short (four or fewer words) and no misreading is likely, the comma may be omitted.

- I felt ill and my friend left.

Rule 4. Introductory Subordinate Clause or Verbal Phrase
Use a comma to separate an introductory subordinate clause or an introductory verbal phrase from an independent clause.

Subordinate Clause:
- Before I took my summer vacation, I broke my thumb.
- If you finish early, you should start on the next case file.

Verbal Phrase:
- Determined to pass the typing test, the job candidate planned many hours of practice.
- Shopping for clothes during lunch, I ran into my previous boss.

Rule 5. Introductory Prepositional Phrase
Use a comma to separate an introductory prepositional phrase from an independent clause.

- In the late evening, we saw Mr. Smith at the bank.
- Upon reaching California, Nancy stopped for lunch.
- Behind the low brick wall, a dog slept in the shade.

The comma may be omitted for a two-word phrase that does not reduce clarity.

Comma May Be Omitted:
- In 1884 tornado deaths dropped by 5 percent.
- After lunch we saw Mr. Smith at the bank.

Comma Needed for Clarity:
- In May, April will graduate from college.
- In 1844, 142 people died from tornados.
  - See Rule 87 for a comma with adjacent numbers.

Rule 6. Introductory Conjunctive Adverb, Transitional Expression, or Parenthetical Expression

Use a comma to separate an introductory conjunctive adverb, transitional expression, or parenthetical expression from an independent clause. Do not place a comma after the conjunctive adverbs *hence, then, thus, so*, and *yet*.

Conjunctive Adverb or Transitional Expression:
- I heard the scream. However, I did not call the police.
- I heard the scream. Thus I called the police.
- I took the medicine. As a result, I fell asleep quickly.

Parenthetical Expression:
- In my opinion, he stole the jewelry.
- I still remember the license plate number after twenty years. Obviously, I have an excellent memory.

When the word *yes, no, okay,* or *well* begins a sentence, separate it with a comma because the word is used as a parenthetical expression. Removing it would not affect the meaning of the sentence.

- Yes, I am a doctor.
- Okay, let's begin the lecture.
- I was asked if I'm a doctor. Well, I am.
- Did he leave work early? No, he did not.

When the word *now* or *then* begins a sentence and it has the meaning of *well*, separate it with a comma. If *now* or *then* relates to time or sequence, do not separate it with a comma.

- Now, that is a point well taken.
- Sam went to the grocery store. Then he got gas.

Rule 7. Nonessential Clause or Phrase
Use a comma (end of sentence) or commas (midsentence) to separate a nonessential subordinate clause, verbal phrase, prepositional phrase, transitional expression, or parenthetical expression.

Nonessential elements are always separated with punctuation, and essential elements are never separated with punctuation. Some midsentence examples may be judged as interrupting the sentence flow, requiring a comma for separation (Rule 9).

Subordinate Clause:
- Pharmco's principal office, which is in Ohio, has an excellent reputation.
- Keith moved to New York in 2013, when he was 23.

Verbal Phrase:
An *-ing* phrase at the end of a sentence is often nonessential.

- They evicted the renter, having failed to collect any rent.
- Sandra applied to Stanford this year, graduating high school last May.
- The 2016 document, written before Tom's death, states his soon-to-be ex-wife borrowed the money.

Prepositional Phrase:
- Linda's condition, on the whole, is improving.
- Linda's condition is improving, on the whole.

Transitional or Parenthetical Expression:
- I studied hard for the exam. The results, however, showed not hard enough.
- I rather not attend the party, to tell you the truth.

Rule 8. Appositives

Use a comma (end of sentence) or commas (midsentence) to separate an appositive adjective or nonessential appositive.

An appositive adjective is an adjective that follows the noun. An appositive is a noun or phrase that renames a preceding noun or pronoun.

Nonessential elements are always separated with punctuation, and essential elements are never separated with punctuation. A useful way to determine an essential appositive from a nonessential appositive is the location of the proper noun (see Rule 61). When an appositive follows a proper noun, the appositive is usually nonessential. When a proper noun is the appositive, it is typically essential.

Nonessential Appositive:
- Dr. Cooper, my psychologist, last saw me on June 12.
- Bizen ware, a dark stoneware, was produced in Japan for centuries.
- High-speed roadways, especially freeways, have higher accident rates.
- My youngest brother, Jack, is an attorney.

Essential Appositive:
- My sister Jane is an attorney.
  - If the person has only one sister, the appositive is nonessential and separate it with commas: "My sister, Jane, is an attorney."
- Was the defendant Mr. Smith home at the time?
  - If the case has only one defendant, the appositive is nonessential and separate it with commas: "Was the defendant, Mr. Smith, home at the time?"

Appositive Adjective:
- Jim was a big boy, tall and strong.
- I love steak, lean and tender, served with a Caesar salad.

Rule 9. Interrupting Word, Phrase, or Clause

Use commas to separate a word, phrase, or clause that interrupts the flow of the sentence.

The interrupting word, phrase, or clause often comes between the subject and the verb.

- The injured victim, because of blood loss, collapsed.
- Mr. Smith, only ten minutes after the meeting, called with the information I requested.
- Ms. Anderson is being sued, so I have been told, by her previous attorney.
- It happened, you know, in the middle of dinner.
- I, like, worry all the time.

Rule 10. Introductory Phrase or Clause Before a Second Independent Clause

When an introductory phrase or clause precedes the second independent clause of a compound sentence, use a comma before the coordinating conjunction and a comma after the introductory phrase or clause. Omit the comma after a one-word conjunctive adverb.

Use a comma before the coordinating conjunction in most cases. Per Rule 20, use a semicolon when a misreading is likely. This typically occurs when

- both independent clauses contain at least one internal comma.
- the introductory element or an independent clause contains multiple internal commas.

Use a Comma:
- We can meet Wednesday afternoon, or if you prefer, we can meet Thursday morning.
- I arrived late to work, and when no one was looking, I snuck into my office.
- Jim spilled coffee on his shirt, and realizing the boss noticed, he excused himself.
- Management promoted Tiffany last week, and to tell you the truth, everyone was relieved it was not Jacob.

One-Word Conjunctive Adverb:
- I arrived late to work, and unfortunately almost everyone noticed.
- We can meet Wednesday afternoon, or otherwise we can meet Thursday morning.

Use a Semicolon:
The first two examples focus on an introductory phrase or clause before a second independent clause in a compound sentence. See Rule 20 for more examples.

- The office supply shipment lacked ordered items; and when I called customer service to send the pens, binders, and paper clips, they had no record of the order.
- Sarah discussed Tom's unprofessional conduct with the manager; and if the situation was not corrected with an email, letter, or meeting, Sarah would contact the union.
- Management, after a quick phone meeting with HR, met with Tom; and understanding Sarah's concerns, Tom realized how to communicate better.

Rule 11. Contrasting Phrases
Use a comma (end of sentence) or commas (midsentence) to separate a contrasting phrase.

Words or phrases beginning a contrasting phrase include *but, even though, never, not, rather, rather than,* and *though.* The comma may be omitted if the contrasting phrase, usually a *but* phrase, does not interrupt the sentence flow.

- Plead for mercy, not justice.
- The staff meeting occurs on Mondays, never Tuesdays.
- They traveled to Chicago on Monday, rather than Tuesday, as the report indicates.
- Diana's vacation was short but enjoyable.

Rule 12. Series of Items

Use commas to separate a series of three or more words, phrases, or clauses. Use a comma before the final item's coordinating conjunction.

The Serial Comma:
A serial or "Oxford" comma is a comma before the final item's coordinating conjunction (and, or, nor). While the comma is not technically required, most style guides highly recommend or require its use (highly recommend: CMOS and GRM; require: MLA and APA). Some style guides, like the AP, only require a serial comma when the meaning would be unclear.

- The training included John, Mary, Bob, and Barbara.
- I went to the store and bought milk, bread, and eggs.
- Josephine said she will not live near the ocean, by a lake, or even next to a pond.
- Randy moved to New York, Frank relocated to San Francisco, and Susan stayed in Chicago.

See Rule 21 if the series contains internal commas.

See Rule 26 if the series begins a sentence.

Comma after Et Cetera a Series of Items:
Only use a comma after *et cetera* (etc.) or a series of items if another punctuation rule requires it. CMOS does not require a comma after *et cetera* and considers the practice "traditional usage." GRM, however, requires a comma after *et cetera*.

- The instructor invited John, Mary, Bob, and Barbara to the employee training.
- My son grabbed his swimsuit, beach towel, et cetera for a trip to the beach.
  - GRM would place a comma after *et cetera*.
- Seeing John, Mary, Bob, and Barbara, the instructor greeted them warmly.
  - Comma after series required per Rule 4.
- When my son grabbed his swimsuit, beach towel, et cetera, he forgot his cellphone.
  - Comma after et cetera required per Rule 4.

All Items in a Series Connected with Conjunctions:
When all the items in the series are connected with coordinating conjunctions (and, or, nor), do not use commas to separate the items.

- I went to the store and bought milk and bread and eggs.
- The training included John and Mary and Bob and Barbara.

The Order of Items in a Series:
The best way to order the items in a series is from short to long. Exceptions include expected order, sequential or chronological order, and the need to avoid a misplaced modifier.

Original:	I ate tangerines, pears, and apples.
Revised:	I ate pears, apples, and tangerines.

Original:	Have you lived in New York; Washington, D.C.; or Miami?
Revised:	Have you lived in Miami; New York; or Washington, D.C.?

Original:	The top reasons for nonpayment are poor material quality and workmanship
Revised:	The top reasons for nonpayment are workmanship and poor material quality.

Original:	I take the medication with lunch, dinner, and breakfast.
Revised:	I take the medication with breakfast, lunch, and dinner. (Chronological order)

Original:	I love cream and peaches.
Revised:	I love peaches and cream. (Expected order)

Rule 13. Coordinate Adjectives
Use a comma to separate two adjectives that equally modify the following noun.

- She bought a sleek, shiny car.
- He has been a faithful, sincere friend.

Adjectives that equally modify the following noun are called coordinate adjectives. They describe the same "quality":

- Opinion (beautiful, fine)
- Size (round, square)
- Age (new, old)
- Color (red, blue)
- Origin (German, American)
- Material (wood, stone)

Coordinate adjectives can answer yes to the following tests:
1. Can "and" be inserted sensibly between the adjectives?
2. Can the adjectives be sensibly reversed?

Example: She bought a **sleek, shiny** car.
- Test 1: She bought a sleek and shiny car. (Yes)
- Test 2: She bought a shiny, sleek car. (Yes)
- Result: *shiny* and *sleek* are coordinate adjectives

Example: He has been a **faithful, sincere** friend.
- Test 1: He has been a faithful and sincere friend. (Yes)
- Test 2: He has been a sincere, faithful friend. (Yes)
- Result: *faithful* and *sincere* are coordinate adjectives

If adjectives are not coordinate adjectives, they are cumulative adjectives because each adjective describes a different quality. Do not separate cumulative adjectives with a comma.

- We saw an **old black** bear.
  - *Old* is an opinion; *black* regards species (origin).

- We ate **German chocolate** cake.
  - *German* regards origin; *chocolate* is a material.

- We bought two **round wooden** tables.
  - *Round* is a shape; *wooden* is a material.

See Rule 46 for determining a compound adjective.

Rule 14. Direct Address
Use a comma (beginning or end of the sentence) or commas (midsentence) to separate names or words used as direct address.

Beginning of the Sentence:
- Mr. Smith, please email the document.
- Angela, did you have lunch with your friends?
- Ladies and gentlemen, we will now break for lunch.

Midsentence:
- With all due respect, Thomas, I disagree.
- Please tell us, Ms. Anderson, where you work.

End of the Sentence:
- I called in sick that day, Michelle.
- Can I count on your support, sir?

Rule 15. Titles and Degrees Following a Personal Name
Use commas to separate titles or degrees following a personal name.

- Ruth Walker, CEO, approved the revised budget.
- We spoke to Mr. Smith, PhD, for more information.
- Mrs. Anderson, Esq., will represent Mr. Smith in the criminal case.

See Rule 93 for not using periods in a title or degree.

Rule 16. Jr. and Sr. Following a Personal Name
Do not separate *Jr.* or *Sr.* following a personal name with commas unless using MLA style or a person prefers it. Never separate a numerical designation following a personal name with commas.

- Robert Smith Sr. graduated high school in 1956.
- Robert Smith Jr. graduated high school in 1982.
- Robert Smith, Jr., graduated high school in 1982.
  - MLA style or the person prefers commas.
- Robert Smith III graduated high school in 2011.

Rule 17. Use of Colon, Dash, Semicolon, and Parentheses

Do not overuse the colon, dash, semicolon, or parentheses.

The popular style guides warn against overusing the colon, dash, semicolon, and parentheses. Use these punctuation marks deliberately and sparingly unless the punctuation mark is required by rule. Consider using a comma or period first.

Rule 18. Independent Clauses Without a Conjunction

A semicolon may separate two closely related independent clauses joined without a coordinating conjunction. Using a period to separate the clauses is always acceptable.

The two independent clauses may be closely related by meaning, content, or grammatical structure. Often the first independent clause creates an expectation, and the second independent clause fulfills it.

- The wallet was not in my purse; my anxiety exploded.
  - or ". . . purse. My . . ."
- The football play caused a large hole in Mark's jersey; he hoped a coach could quickly repair it.
  - or ". . . jersey. Mark . . ."
- The newspaper headline emphasized the dramatic outcome; the article contained the mundane details causing the event.
  - or ". . . outcome. The . . ."

Rule 19. Independent Clauses with Conjunctive Adverb or Transitional Expression

A semicolon may separate two independent clauses joined with a conjunctive adverb or transitional expression. Using a period to separate the clauses is always acceptable.

Place a comma after a conjunctive adverb (however, therefore) or transitional expression (for example). Do not place a comma after *hence, then, thus, so*, and *yet.*

- I heard the scream; however, I did not call the police.
  - or ". . . scream. However, I . . ."
- I heard the scream; thus I called the police.
  - or ". . . scream. Thus I . . ."
- I took the medicine; as a result, I fell asleep quickly.
  - or ". . . medicine. As a result, I . . ."

Rule 20. Independent Clauses with Internal Commas

Use a semicolon to separate two independent clauses joined with a coordinating conjunction when a misreading is likely because of internal commas. Using a period to separate the clauses is always acceptable.

A misreading typically occurs when

- both independent clauses contain at least one internal comma.
- an introductory element or an independent clause contains multiple internal commas.

Misreading Because of Internal Commas:
The following examples focus on independent clauses in a compound sentence containing internal commas. See Rule 10 for more examples.

- I ordered pens, pencils, and paper; and I had them mailed express delivery.
- When I woke up, I saw the assailant with a knife in their hand; and if I had regained consciousness a few moments later, I would be dead.
- We can meet Wednesday afternoon; or if you prefer, we can meet Thursday morning, Friday afternoon, or Monday morning.

Strong Break:
Use a semicolon between two independent clauses joined with a coordinating conjunction when a stronger-than-comma break is needed or desired for clarity (see Rule 3). Often both clauses are long and the sentence exceeds twenty-five words.

- Susan guaranteed the large personal loan for the kitchen remodel with her expensive sports car; but the bank's loan officer denied the loan application without even contacting her.
- Many people think they could solve society's problems if given the power; but people usually lack a coherent or detailed plan that may be objectively evaluated.

Rule 21. Series of Items with Internal Commas

Use semicolons to separate a series of three or more phrases or clauses containing internal commas.

- I have lived in Cincinnati, Ohio; Seattle, Washington; and Santa Cruz, California.
- She paid rent of $1,500 on April 2, 2017; $1,300 on May 1, 2017; and only $200 on June 16, 2017.
- The attendance figures arrived at 10 p.m.: Zone 1, 233; Zone 2, 132; Zone 3, 265; and Zone 4, 118.

<u>The Colon:</u>

Rule 22. Independent Clause Followed by a Series, Appositive, or Explanation

Use a colon to separate an independent clause from a following series, appositive, or explanation.

An independent clause always precedes a colon. However, a word, phrase, series, or sentence may follow a colon. Use a colon after an independent clause when followed by

- a series.
- an appositive.
- an explanatory independent clause.

Series:

- I shipped a box full of books on different topics: math, science, and history.
- The steps are as follows: call for an incident number, fill out the online application, and send a confirmation email.

Appositive:
- I attend only one type of music festival: jazz.
- Junk food has two huge disadvantages: fat and calories.

Explanation:
A period or semicolon may also be appropriate.

- The local "laws" are different: you are guilty unless proven innocent.
  - or ". . . different. You . . ."
  - or ". . . different; you . . ."
- I have two observations about this witness that will hurt the case: the previous perjury and the criminal record.
  - or ". . . case. The . . ."
  - or ". . . case; the . . ."

See Rule 30 for a colon before a question within a sentence.

See Rule 33 for a colon before a direct quotation.

Rule 23. Capitalization after a Colon
Capitalize the first word after a colon when the word is a proper noun, when two or more related sentences follow, or when one or more sentences follow that require special emphasis.

AP and APA capitalize the first word following a colon if one or more sentences follow, not two sentences. Per the popular style guides, "special emphasis" includes the statement of a rule or principle.

- I have two observations about this witness that will hurt the case: Brandon's previous perjury and his criminal record.
- The local "laws" are different: First, you are guilty unless proven innocent. Second, the sheriff is always right.
- George was in a difficult situation: He could lie and escape embarrassment, but feel guilty. Or he could tell the uncomfortable truth.
- Here is a fundamental punctuation rule: Nonessential elements are always separated with punctuation.

<u>The Dash</u>:

Rule 24. Abrupt Break and Afterthoughts
Use a dash to separate an abrupt break in thought or an afterthought at the end of a sentence.

Abrupt Break:
- Ethan exited his truck and jogged—ran to the overturned car engulfed in flames.
- Olivia asked me—her husband was away on business—to watch her two young children.

Afterthought:
- DiMaggio's has the best pizza in town—and maybe the fastest delivery.
- Many things changed this year—mostly for the better.

Rule 25. Sentence Element with Internal Commas
A dash may separate a sentence element that contains internal commas and requires separation with punctuation.

- We—Tom, Sue, and Bill—formed the legal team for the prominent client.
- The witness—reluctant, soft-spoken, and nervous—described a single suspect.

The sentence element is usually nonessential. If the break with dashes is too strong, consider using parentheses (Rule 48).

Rule 26. Series at the Beginning of a Sentence
Use a dash after a series of items at the beginning of a sentence.

- Tom, Sue, and Bill—we formed the legal team for the prominent client.
- Reluctant, soft-spoken, and nervous—the witness described a single suspect.

Rule 27. Emphatic Substitution for a Comma, Colon, Parentheses, or Semicolon

A dash may be used as an emphatic substitute for a comma, colon, parentheses, or semicolon.

The dash creates a strong break and emphasizes the following sentence element. Emphatic substitution for a comma, colon, parentheses, or semicolon should be infrequent and deliberate.

Substitute for the Comma:
- Linda's condition—contrary to her brother's text message—is improving.
- The information I sent is correct—and you know it.

Substitute for the Colon:
- Brandon has two big problems hurting the case—the previous perjury and a criminal record.
- I shipped a letter with the important documents—birth certificate, marriage certificate, and vehicle title.

Substitute for the Semicolon:
- I counted all the face masks—there are only fifty left.
- We must finish the job—it must be comprehensive and accurate.

Substitute for Parentheses:
- The witness—reluctant, soft-spoken, and nervous—described a single suspect.
- The Atlanta sales team—we consistently outperform them—thinks they finally beat us.

The Question Mark:

Rule 28. Direct Question
Use a question mark after a direct question.

- What time do you leave work?
- Did Zoey see the recent survey results?
- Luis asked if Melinda will attend the meeting.
  - Use a period with an indirect question.

Use a question mark after a grammatically incomplete direct question that represents a complete question. The missing grammatical elements are understood from the context.

- When will that assignment be finished? In a day or two?
- At the time of the accident, were you walking? Jogging? Running?

Rule 29. Short Question Within a Sentence

Use a comma (end of sentence) or commas (midsentence) to separate a short direct question of three or fewer words within a sentence. Place the question mark at the end of the sentence.

The short direct question, especially in informal writing, may be grammatically incomplete. A period may separate a short and grammatically complete question at the end of a sentence.

- Angela, can't she, drop off the report tomorrow?
- Mr. Smith had leg surgery, didn't he, before 2015?

- Angela dropped off the report, didn't she?
- Mr. Smith had leg surgery before 2015, right?
- You are traveling to Texas, is that correct?
  - Also: You are traveling to Texas. Is that correct?

Use dashes to separate a long midsentence question of four or more words. Place the question mark before the closing dash.

- The client's file—does the manager want a copy?—will answer all the questions.
- The couple tried—did they not try their best?—to find the lost dog.

Rule 30. Long Question After an Opening Phrase

Use a comma to separate a long question of four or more words that follows an opening phrase. Capitalize the first word of the question.

The opening phrase frequently ends with *is, are, was,* and *were.*

- The key question in the report was, Did the data confirm the hypotheses?
- The question is, Did you see the news report?
- Randell thought, What am I doing here?
- Local government leaders debated, How can we fund important services with limited funding?

When the long question follows an independent clause, use a colon to separate the question.

- The report had one key question: Did the data confirm the hypotheses?
- The question is this: Did you see the news report?
- Local government leaders debated the topic: How to fund important services with limited funding?

When the phrase follows the question, place a question mark after the question and do not capitalize the phrase.

- Did the data confirm the hypotheses? was the key question in the report.
- Did you see the news report? is the question.
- How can we fund important services with limited funding? debated local government leaders.

<u>Quotation Marks</u>*:*

Rule 31. Direct Quotation
Enclose a direct quotation in double quotation marks. Capitalize the first word of a direct quotation when it is a proper noun, a proper adjective, begins a sentence, or begins a line of poetry.

- She said, "Bill, not Amy, illegally accessed the checking and savings account."
- James replied, "Who said that lie?"
- The report states this: "Officer Ramirez arrived at 7:34 a.m. After the homeowner was contacted, he searched the backyard."

Use single quotation marks for a direct quotation within a direct quotation.

- Leon explained his nervousness, "Lisa said, 'Don't dare run into me at party.'"
- The teacher said, "Let's dive into the context of the well-known phrase 'Letting someone off the hook.'"

The Quotation section has formatting and other information about direct quotations (see page 130).

Rule 32. Signal Phrases with Direct Quotations

Separate an introductory, interrupting, or concluding "signal phrase" from a direct quotation with commas (see examples). Omit the comma if a period, question mark, or exclamation point occurs where the comma would be placed.

Signal phrases include the verbs *said, asked, responded, stated, replied, yelled, screamed,* and similar verbs.

Introductory Signal Phrase:
See Rule 33 for a colon before a direct quotation.

- The manager said, "It's time to go."
- Tammy emailed, "I will fly to New York on Friday."
- Anya yelled, "Get out of here," and she dashed out of the conference room.
- The attorney asked, "Do you know her?" and pointed to the defendant.
  - Comma omitted after *her* due to the question mark.

Concluding Signal Phrase:
- "It's time to go," the manager said.
- "Who said that lie?" James asked.
  - Comma omitted after *lie* due to the question mark.

Interrupting Signal Phrase:
- "I'm traveling," Tom whispered, "to Chicago for business next week."

- "I really like the plan," Mary replied. "However, I have a few changes."
  - o Comma omitted after *replied* due to the period.

No Signal Phrase:
- I disagree with Liam that we are just "evolved animals."
- The medical reference states "minimal side effects" with that dosage.

Rule 33. Colon Before Direct Quotation

Use a colon before a direct quotation when an independent clause introduces the direct quotation or when the direct quotation is more than one sentence.

- The judge gave the jury excellent instructions: "Gather the facts and decide the case in the deliberation room."
- I will always remember my father's advice: "Always do what you think is right."
- Mrs. Anderson said: "I have heard enough, and you are beating around the bush. Please answer the question."

Rule 34. Closing Quotation Marks with Other Punctuation

Always place a period or comma inside closing quotation marks, and always place a colon or semicolon outside closing quotation marks. Place all other punctuation marks outside the closing quotation marks unless it is part of the original quote.

AP places a colon or semicolon inside the closing quotation marks when it is part of the direct quotation. CMOS, GRM, MLA, and APA always place a colon or semicolon outside closing quotation marks.

Period and Comma:
- Lester shouted, "Hold the elevator."
- Mary used satire in her poem "Scorned."
- I recall saying, "It's a simple sentence."
- "Hold the elevator," he shouted.
- "It is a simple sentence," I recall saying.

Semicolon and Colon:
- Customer service did not honor the "no hassle warranty"; I emailed the company president that day.
- The company motto was "Efficiency"; now it is "Simplicity."
- In customer service calls, we include two things under "other": service visits and phone conversations.
- The survey concluded "the number one reason people use incorrect punctuation": too many rules to remember.

Punctuation Part of the Original Quote:
- "Do you want your receipt?" She asked.
- She asked, "Did you sign the agreement?"
- The text message read, "Watch out!"
- The police report states, "I saw a hooded person—"

Punctuation Not Part of the Original Quote:
- Who first yelled "fire"?
- Did Lester say, "Hold the elevator"?
- Mia overheard the gang member say, "let's murder"—
- The tree trimmer shouted, "Timber"!

Rule 35. Titles of Book Chapters, Magazine Articles, Songs and Poems

Use quotation marks to enclose the title of a work within a larger work: book chapter, magazine article, newspaper article, song from an album, poem in a book, TV episode, web page, blog post, and so on. Also, use quotation marks to enclose the title of an unpublished work.

- Have you read the magazine article "Heart Disease: Just the Facts"?
- My favorite *Twilight Zone* episode is "To Serve Man."
- Judy Garland sings "Somewhere over the Rainbow" from *The Wizard of Oz*.

Italicize the title of a book, magazine, newspaper, movie, TV series, music album, website, or blog (Rule 58).

Rule 36. Special Emphasis

Use quotation marks for special emphasis to show a word or phrase is used in an unusual, unfamiliar, or technical way. Use quotation marks with only the first occurrence.

Do not use quotation marks with words introduced by *so-called*.

- Some called it a tax. I called it "revenue augmentation."
- I told him to "solve" the problem.
- What does "final approval" include?
- The so-called training came across as a sales pitch.

<u>The Apostrophe</u>*:*

Rule 37. Possessive of Singular and Plural Word

To form the possessive of a singular word, add an apostrophe and *s*. To form the possessive of a plural word ending in *s*, add an apostrophe. To form the possessive of a plural word not ending in *s*, add an apostrophe and *s*.

Singular Word:
- The defendant's testimony is pure perjury.
- Andrew borrowed his friend's car to get to work.
- The business's profit dropped sharply last month.
- Tess's expense report is detailed and accurate.

Except for CMOS and MLA, many style guides allow proper names that are singular in meaning which end in *s* to form the possessive with only an apostrophe.

- Thieves stole Joan Rivers' car.
- Scholars debate the size of Xerxes' invasion army.
  - CMOS and MLA: Xerxes's invasion army

Plural Word Ending in "s":
- The profit did not meet investors' expectations.
- The email violated the employees' computer policy.

Plural Word Not Ending in "s":
- The next school board meeting will discuss children's educational needs and requirements.
- Is women's intuition a myth or reality?

To show separate possession, use the possessive form with each item or person.

- Rebecca's and Mason's drawing technique is similar.
  - Each person has a separate, yet similar, drawing technique.
- Todd joined the fraternity against his mother's and his father's repeated advice.
  - The mother and father had separate advice, though both were against Todd joining the fraternity. Repeating *his* reinforces separate possession.

To show joint or common possession, use the possessive form with only the final item or person.

- Rebecca and Mason's large drawing is in the art exhibit.
  - They jointly produced the large drawing.
- Todd joined the fraternity against his mother and father's repeated advice.
  - The parents had the same or common advice.

Rule 38. Possessive or Descriptive Word?

To determine if a word is a possessive or descriptive word, rewrite as an *of* phrase and as a *for* phrase. If the *of* phrase better matches the meaning, use an apostrophe. If the *for* phrase better matches the meaning, do not use an apostrophe.

- The **Reynolds** car OR the **Reynolds'** car?
  - Rewrite with *of:* car of the Reynolds. (Yes)
  - Rewrite with *for:* car for the Reynolds. (No)
  - Conclusion: Reynolds'. (Possessive)

- New **leaders** guide OR new **leaders'** guide?
  - Rewrite with *of:* guide of new leaders. (Possible)
  - Rewrite with *for:* guide for new leaders. (Most likely)
  - Conclusion: leaders. (Descriptive)

- The **girls** softball team OR the **girls'** softball team?
  - Rewrite with *of:* softball team of girls. (Most likely)
  - Rewrite with *for:* softball team for girls. (Possible)
  - Conclusion: girls'. (Possessive)

Rule 39. Plural of Lowercase Letter or Likely Misread Word

Use an apostrophe and *s* to form the plural of a lowercase letter or the plural of any word likely to be misread.

Lowercase Letter:
- Please mind your *p*'s and *q*'s.
- You spelled the word with one too many *t*'s.
- Wilber had two *x*'s in red ink across his face.

Form the plural of an uppercase letter by adding *s*. However, AP and MLA use apostrophe and *s*.
- The word is misspelled. It contains two Ts.
    - AP and MLA: ". . . two T's."
- Wilber had two Xs in red ink across his face.
    - AP and MLA: ". . . two X's . . ."

Word Likely to Be Misread:
- The or's in the sentence should be ands.
- In the company motto, the that's could be deleted.

Per the *Merriam-Webster.com Dictionary,* the correct spelling of some common phrases are as follows:
- ands, ifs, and buts
- dos and don'ts
    - AP: do's and don'ts
- ins and outs
- yeses and nos

Rule 40. Omission of Letters or Figures

Use an apostrophe to show omitted letters or figures.

- My son was born in '97.
- I bought the condo in 2011 or '12.
- I love rock 'n' roll.
- Have you tried Shake 'n Bake chicken?
    - Follow the official product spelling.

See Rule 86 for formatting a number range.

Rule 41. To Form Certain Verbs
Use an apostrophe before the suffix of a letter, number, or abbreviation to form a verb.

- The manager just ok'd the travel expense.
- The investigation showed the person OD'd Friday night.
- The detective star 69'd the landline phone to reach the last-called person.
- Jan is sick, so she x'd her European vacation.

In formal writing, use the verb's full form or use a different verb. For example, use *okayed* (not ok'd) in first example and *canceled* (not x'd) in the last example.

While a dictionary may have a verb form with a hyphen or without an apostrophe, it always includes the apostrophe form. The *Merriam-Webster.com Dictionary* has the following entries:

cc'd	cc'ing
ID'd, IDed	ID'ing, IDing
OD'd, ODed	OD'ing (and OD's)
OK'd, ok'd	OK'ing, ok'ing
x'd, x-ed, xed	x'ing, x-ing

<u>The Hyphen</u>*:*

Rule 42. Common Prefixes and Suffixes
Add most prefixes and suffixes without a hyphen to form a closed word.

Prefix:
- The accident occurred **midblock**.
- What did the **postmortem** reveal?

Attach the prefixes *ex-* (meaning *former*) and *self-* with a hyphen (ex-convict, ex-husband, self-serving, self-worth).

Suffix:
- The wind moved the tall grass in a **wavelike** motion.
- What are the new **statewide** laws?

Rule 43. Prefix to a Number, Capitalized Word, or a Word That Might Be Misread

Use a hyphen to join a prefix to a number, capitalized word, or a word that might be misread.

Capitalized Word:
- Political leaders rejected the anti-American policy.
- The article summarized post-NAFTA economics.
- Is the Memphis-wide music festival in August?
  - Also hyphenate suffixes to capitalized words.

Number:
- Where is the pre-1900 machine exhibit?
- The graph shows the post-2008 market recovery.

A Word That Might Be Misread:
- The **ultra-apathetic** student unplugged the alarm clock.
  - A double *a* combination requires a hyphen.

- My doctor suggested an **anti-inflammatory** medication.
  - A double *i* combination requires a hyphen.

- The water is **un-ionized**.
  - A hyphen is required because *unionized* has a different meaning.

- Do we need to **re-create** the scene?
  - A hyphen is required because *recreate* has a different meaning. Other examples beginning with the prefix *re-* are common.

- The requirement is in the **sub-subparagraph**.
  - A doubled prefix requires a hyphen.

- The ad stated it was "**post-self-cleaning**."
  - A prefix to a hyphenated word requires a hyphen.

- The list had successful **non-high school** graduates.
  - A prefix to an open compound requires a hyphen. MLA hyphenates the prefix and open compound (non-high-school graduates).

- The new employee was eager but **skill-less**.
  - A suffix with tripled consonants requires a hyphen. Common situations include *-less* and *-like*.

Rule 44. Suspending Hyphens
Use a suspending hyphen with each prefix, suffix, word, or number that applies to the following (or preceding) hyphenated word.

- I bought certified deposits for 12- and 24-month terms.
- Alexia has 9-, 11-, and 14-year-old children.
- My pre- and post-op anxiety levels were off the chart.
- I would guess George is twenty-one or -two.

Rule 45. Compound Words
Check a dictionary to determine if a compound noun, compound adjective, or compound verb is open, hyphenated, or closed. If the word is not listed in the dictionary, consult similar entries.

Many style guides use *Merriam-Webster's Collegiate Dictionary*.

Compound Noun:
Use an open compound noun if not listed in the dictionary.

- I selected **African American** on the application form.
  - Write a compound nationality as an open compound.
- Angela did a **run-through** of the new computer system.
- My **brother-in-law** is a **know-it-all**.
- I currently work as a **stockbroker**.
- The job listing is for a **schoolteacher**.

Compound Verb:
Many compound verbs are hyphenated or closed.

- The thief **strong-armed** my purse from me.
- Did you **test-drive** the car before buying it?
- I **downloaded** the latest software update.
- She **proofread** the third draft of the book.

Compound Adjective:
See Rule 46 and Rule 47 for guidance on compound adjectives.

- I work in the **high-rise** building on Main Street.
- She invented a **time-saving** gadget.
- I attended many **high school** dances.
- My retirement funds are in a **money market** account.

Rule 46. Identifying a Compound Adjective

If the words before a noun work as a unit to express a single idea, they form a compound adjective. Consult a dictionary to determine if the compound adjective is open, hyphenated, or closed.

See Rule 13 about coordinating and cumulative adjectives.

Compound Adjective Test:
To determine if the words "work as a unit," check them jointly and separately with the noun. Does each word by itself sensibly modify the noun? Do the joined words form a single idea and sensibly modify the noun? Use these two useful tests in identifying a compound adjective.

- Brad Pitt is a **well known** actor.
    - <u>Words modify separately</u>? No for "well actor." Yes for "known actor."
    - <u>Words modify together</u>? Yes, "well known" expresses a single idea modifying the noun.
    - <u>Conclusion</u>: compound adjective.
    - <u>Dictionary</u>: hyphenated (well-known)

- I live on the eighth floor in a **ten story** building.
    - <u>Words modify separately</u>? No for "ten building." No for "story building."
    - <u>Words modify together</u>? Yes, "ten story" expresses a single idea modifying the noun.
    - <u>Conclusion</u>: compound adjective
    - <u>Dictionary</u>: hyphenated (ten-story)

- The report covers the effects of **second hand** smoke.
    - <u>Words modify separately</u>? No for "second smoke." No for "hand smoke."
    - <u>Words modify together</u>? Yes, "second hand" expresses a single idea modifying the noun.
    - <u>Conclusion</u>: compound adjective
    - <u>Dictionary</u>: closed (secondhand)

Compound adjectives that are long or that could be misread are enclosed in quotation marks.

- Her "I'm going out of my freaking mind" expression scared me.
- His head did a slow "you cannot make me do it" shake.
- Our conversation began with "how was your day?" stuff.

Rule 47. Compound Adjective Not in the Dictionary
When a compound adjective is not listed in the dictionary, hyphenate it unless it includes (1) an adverb ending in *-ly*; (2) a proper noun; (3) the adverb *more, most, less, least,* or *very*; (4) a chemical term; (5) a percentage; (6) a foreign phrase; or (7) a second element consisting of a number or letter.

Adverb Ending in *-ly:*
- Sophia is a **highly valued** employee.
- Is this a **poorly written** sentence?
- Logan joined the **newly formed** business.

Proper Noun:
- The deal took a **New York** minute.
- The **Supreme Court** decision will be issued tomorrow.
- Peter studies **Middle Eastern** languages at Yale.

Adverbs *More, Most, Less, Least,* or *Very:*
- I cannot decide who is the **more determined** person.
- Is punctuation the **least interesting** topic?
- Hailey's **very thoughtful** comment emphasized the immediate needs and how everyone could help.

Chemical Term:
- A **sodium chloride** solution ruined my pants.
- The **amino acid** reaction created a salt.

A Percentage:
- The March 2020 stay-at-home order caused a **50 percent** reduction in traffic.
- Clinical trials showed the medication caused a **10 percent** increase in blood pressure.

Foreign Phrase:
If the original foreign phrase contains hyphens, keep them.
See Rule 59 for using italics with unfamiliar foreign phrases.

- An *a priori* argument is deductive.
- The couple saved for the cost of **in vitro** fertilization.
- Mom and Dad used a ***tête-à-tête*** approach for family finances.

Second Element Consisting of a Number or Letter:
See Rule 89 for numbered references.

- Liam wears a **size 10** shoe.
- Nearly 10 percent of Americans have **Type 2** diabetes.
- Did all **Group B** participants sign the waiver?

Parentheses:

Rule 48. Sentence Element with Internal Commas
Parentheses may separate a sentence element that contains internal commas and requires separation with punctuation.

While the sentence element is usually nonessential, use parentheses when dashes are too strong of a break or when commas would be confusing (Rule 25 and Rule 27).

- We (Tom, Sue, and Bill) formed the legal team for the prominent client.
- The witness (reluctant, soft-spoken, and nervous) described a single suspect.
- In major three cities (Chicago, Detroit, and New York), crime decreased last quarter.

Rule 49. Sentence Element Not Grammatically Related
Use parentheses when a word, number, phrase, or clause is not grammatically related to the sentence. This often occurs with a parenthetical comment, in-text citation or reference, definition of an abbreviation, or a run-in list.

Parenthetical Comment:

- Our west coast office is in Springfield (Oregon).
- Evictions normally take sixty (60) days to process.
- By Friday (perhaps Monday), the job will be completed.
- The Atlanta sales team (we consistently outperform them) thinks they finally beat us.
- I am quitting my job (and I mean it)!
- I fell asleep in the afternoon sun. (I routinely forgot sunblock back then.)
  - For a parenthetical comment at the end of a sentence consisting of a short independent clause, capitalize it and place the period inside the closing parenthesis. Essentially, the parenthetical comment is a separate sentence enclosed in parentheses.

In-Text Citation or Reference:
See Appendix C for in-text source citations.

- The effects of verbal abuse are immense (Jones 2013).
- Do not overuse parentheses (Rule 17).

Definition of an Abbreviation:
See Rule 91 for defining an abbreviation.

- Who is the company's public information officer (PIO)?
- *The Chicago Manual of Style* (CMOS) is a widely used and comprehensive style guide.

Run-In List:
Enclose the numbers or lowercase letters that separate run-in list items in parentheses. Numbers are typically used unless the run-in list is in APA style or is part of a numbered list.

- Capitalize after a colon if (1) the word is a proper noun, (2) two or more related sentences follow, or (3) one or more sentences follow that require special emphasis.
  - APA style would use lowercase letters.

- 2. The applicant forgot to provide the following information: (a) contact phone number, (b) copy of an academic degree, and (c) three references.
  - Run-in list is part of a numbered list.

The List section has information on vertical lists (see page 121).

Back-to-Back Parentheses:
Avoid back-to-back parentheses. Enclose unrelated information in back-to-back parentheses separated by a space, or enclose unrelated information in a single set of parentheses separated by a semicolon. Enclose related information in a single set of parentheses separated by a semicolon.

- Many scholars have commented on this Hebrew word in Isaiah chapter 7 (almah) (Walsh 2009).
    o Unrelated material (Option 1).
- Many scholars have commented on this Hebrew word in Isaiah chapter 7 (almah; Walsh 2009).
    o Unrelated material (Option 2).
- Psychologists recently studied secondary effects of verbal abuse (Jones 2013; Smith 2016).
    o Related material.

Parentheses Within Parentheses:
Use brackets for parentheses within parentheses.

- The Atlanta sales team (we outperformed them last month [July]) thinks they beat us.
- The most comprehensive style guide (*The Chicago Manual of Style* [abbreviated CMOS]) sells used for $50.

Brackets*:*

Rule 50. Changes or Additions to Direct Quotes
Use brackets to enclose a change, addition, or comment within a direct quotation.

- Margie said, "My [warm] smile always breaks the ice."
- The website states, "Fatigue is a common MS [Multiple Sclerosis] symptom."
- "I married that year [2017]," Cody replied.
- "The co-partners [Jobs and Wozniak] founded Apple Computer Company in 1976."

AP uses parentheses instead of brackets.

See page 133 for more information about changes, additions, or comments within a direct quotation.

<u>The Ellipsis</u>:

Rule 51. Omitted Material within a Direct Quotation
Use an ellipsis to show omitted material within a direct quotation. Add a period before an ellipsis to show the words before and after the ellipsis form a complete sentence, even if parts of the sentences are omitted.

Do not use an ellipsis before the first word of a quotation or after the last word of a quotation unless the sentence is in MLA style or is intentionally left incomplete.

Write an ellipsis as three spaced periods with a space before and after the ellipsis. AP writes an ellipsis as three closed periods with a space before and after the ellipsis. APA allows either style.

- "The accident was caused by . . . the defendant."
  - AP: "by … the"
- "The contract term . . . shall be . . . four years from the date of approval."
  - AP: "term … shall be … four"
- "The accident was caused by driver error. . . . In this case, the evidence points to the defendant."
  - Complete sentences before and after the ellipsis.
  - AP: "error. … In"
- "The contract term is four years. . . . Extensions shall not exceed one year."
  - Complete sentences before and after the ellipsis.
  - AP: "years. … Extensions"

Ellipsis at End of Direct Quotation:
- The paragraph begins, "The contract term is . . ."
  - The sentence is intentionally incomplete.
- The paragraph begins, "The contract term is four years."
  - Do not use an ellipsis at the end of a quote (above).
  - MLA (without source citation): "four years. . . ."
  - MLA (with source citation): "four years . . ." (Smith 47).

The Quotation section contains more information on formatting direct quotations (see page 130).

Rule 52. Fragmented or Incomplete Speech
Use an ellipsis to show fragmented or incomplete speech.

- "I . . . I left for . . . lunch, no dinner that evening."
- "But . . . but . . .," Linda mumbled.
- "We were just trying to . . ."
  - AP: "We were just trying to—"

Use a dash to show an interruption (Rule 24).

The Slash:

Rule 53. Separate Alternatives or Lines of Poetry
Use a slash to separate alternatives or lines of poetry.

Other names for the slash include the slant, virgule, or forward slash. The slash is also used with dates (Rule 77), fractions (Rule 84), and two-year date ranges (Rule 86).

Alternates:
Do not use a space before or after a slash unless an alternative is an open compound (see last example).

- The classic car had the original AM/FM tuner.
- Tammy screamed into the phone, quote/unquote, "I don't live there anymore."
- The menu offered the choice of soup and/or salad.
- Both countries dispute the east/west border.
- My father loved the Korean War / Vietnam War exhibit.

Avoid using a slash by replacing it with "and" or "or" based on the context. If the paired terms function as an adjective, a hyphen may be a better choice. From the above examples

- rewrite "soup and/or salad" as "soup or salad."
- rewrite "east/west border" as "east-west border."
- rewrite "Korean War / Vietnam War" as "Korean War and Vietnam War."

Lines of Poetry:
Use one space before and after the slash.

- Robert Frost penned, "The woods are lovely, dark, and deep, / But I have promises to keep."
- Robert Frost wrote, "Home is the place where, when you have to go there / They have to take you in."

If a stanza break falls with a direct quotation, use two slashes with one space before and after the slashes (//).

Rule 54. Period, Question Mark, and Exclamation Mark
Use no space before and one space after a period, question mark, or exclamation mark.

However, use no space after the above punctuation marks when followed by a closing parenthesis or closing quotation mark. Use no space after a decimal point.

- I fell asleep in the afternoon sun. (I routinely forgot sunblock back then.)
- The bus had a flat tire! Did the children arrive at school on time? No, they did not. The bus arrived at 9:30 a.m.
- Lynn asked, "What time does the next ferry leave?"
- At the last weight loss meeting, I lost 2.3 pounds.

With a monospaced font (`typewriter-like font`), use two spaces after a period, question mark, or exclamation mark.

Rule 55. Comma, Colon, and Semicolon
Use no space before and one space after a comma, colon, or semicolon.

However, use no space after a comma within a number ($1,000) or when followed by a closing quotation mark. Use no space after a colon with an expression of time (9:30 a.m.), with a ratio (2:3), between the volume and page number of a book series (*Computer Networks* 3:174), or between the chapter and verse of the Bible (Genesis 1:1).

- Before you mail the package, please stop at the bank and withdraw $1,000.
- "A ferry will cross the river in an hour," Lynn said.
- The children arrived at school around 9:30 a.m.; the bus had a flat tire.
- I dislike one thing: mean people.
- Mix the powder and water in a 5:2 ratio.
- The authors did not fully explain why they quoted Genesis 1:1 in *Computer Networks* 3:174.

With a monospaced font (`typewriter-like font`), use one space after a comma, colon, or semicolon. Traditionally, two spaces followed a colon in a monospaced font.

Rule 56. Dash, Slash, and Hyphen

Use no space before or after a dash, slash, or hyphen.

However, one space follows a suspending hyphen (Rule 44). Use one space before and after a slash when an alternative is an open compound or when separating lines of poetry (Rule 53).

- The punctuation videos are a win-win solution.
- He said, quote/unquote: "Fire. Get out."
- The affected nations—the U.S., Canada, and Mexico—signed the trade agreement.

With a monospaced font (`typewriter-like font`), write the dash as two connected hyphens with no space before and after the hyphens (`--`).

Rule 57. Quotation Marks, Parentheses, and Brackets

Use one space before and no space after an opening quotation mark, opening parenthesis, or opening bracket. Use no space before and one space after a closing quotation mark, closing parenthesis, or closing bracket.

However, use no space after a closing quotation mark, closing parenthesis, or closing bracket when another punctuation mark immediately follows.

- Did he really say, "I love you"?
- The eviction notice has an error: "sixty (30)" days.
- "I married that year [2017]," Cody replied.

<u>Style Overview</u>:
The Gregg Reference Manual contains 104 pages of punctuation rules. *The Chicago Manual of Style* has only half that amount, and the other popular style guides contain much less information.

The Chicago Manual of Style contains comprehensive coverage of key style elements: grammar, spelling, capitalization, number formatting, abbreviations, and italics. While the information on style in *The Gregg Reference Manual* is robust, the material in other popular style guides ranges from minimal to a quarter of the information contained in *The Gregg Reference Manual*.

Rules in the popular style guides often match or mirror *The Chicago Manual of Style* or *The Gregg Reference Manual*. For example, the MLA Style Center (online) regularly cites *The Chicago Manual of Style*.

Reference[a]	Punctuation (pages)	Style[b] (pages)	Source Citation (pages)
Chicago	47	260	178
Gregg	104	199	35
MLA Handbook[c]	21	56	181
APA Manual	11	40	68
AP Stylebook	13	12[d]	0

[a] See Introduction or page 42.

[b] Includes grammar, spelling, capitalization, number formatting, abbreviations, and italics. Not included are formatting lists, tables, and quotations; word usage; document formatting; and so on.

[c] The MLA Style Center (https://style.mla.org/) has additional articles on punctuation and style.

[d] The AP Stylebook is primarily a word usage and information resource.

<u>Italics</u>:

Rule 58. Title of a Published, Produced, or Released Work
Italicize the title of a published, produced, or released work, especially the title of a work consisting of smaller units.

book	movie	website	music album
magazine	TV series	blog	opera
newspaper	radio show	podcast series	play
journal	DVD	painting	musical
report	video	drawing	ballet
pamphlet	software	photograph	
speech	video game	statue	

- I published my first book, *The Court Reporter's Reference of Realtime Conflicts*, in November 2012.
- The article Mr. Sanchez quoted may be found in the *New York Times*, Section B, page 4.
- My favorite *Twilight Zone* episode is "To Serve Man."

CMOS does not italicize the titles of software, and GRM does not italicize the titles of software or video games.

AP encloses a title in quotation marks because it does not italicize words. It also does not use quotation marks with the titles of software, video games, or reference works (almanac, dictionary, encyclopedia).

See Rule 64 for capitalization of a published, produced, or released work.

Enclose the title of a work within a larger work in quotation marks: book chapter, newspaper article, magazine article, TV episode, song from an album, web page, blog post, podcast episode (Rule 35).

Rule 59. Word Definition or Unfamiliar Foreign Word
Italicize a word or phrase being formally defined, and enclose the definition in quotation marks. Also, italicize an unfamiliar foreign word or phrase, and enclose any translation in quotation marks or parentheses.

- The editorial did not reflect the *vox populi*.
- *La citudad y los perros*, literally translated "the city and the dogs," was published in 1963 with the title *The Time of the Hero*.
- Scholars think the Prakrit word *majjao* (tomcat) derives from two earlier Sanskrit words.
- In this policy section, *schedule* means "a written or printed list, catalog, or inventory."

Do not italicize foreign words listed in the dictionary unless it is unfamiliar to the audience. AP does not italicize words; it encloses the defined or translated words in quotation marks.

Italicize a word used as a word (which may be introduced by the phrase *the word*) or a lowercase letter used as a letter.

- Do not search for the word *punctuation* in this book.
- Please mind your *p*'s and *q*'s.

Rule 60. Genes and Scientific Names of Plants and Animals
Italicize a symbol or an abbreviation of a gene name. Also, italicize the Latin name of a species and subspecies for plants and animals.

Species and Subspecies:
A species name is a two-part name comprised of the capitalized genus name and the lowercase species name. Any abbreviation for the words *subspecies* or *variety* (subsp., ssp., var., or f.) before the subspecies is not italicized.

- When Neanderthals (*Homo neanderthalensis*) split with modern humans (*Homo sapiens*) is unclear.
- *Natrix helvetica* became a separate species in 2017.
- *Schoenoplectus californicus* subsp. *tatora* is a notable plant found on Lake Titicaca.

Capitalize the Latin name of a plant or animal (Rule 70).

Gene:
- Human genes include *IGH* (immunoglobulin heavy).
- *GIF* (gastric intrinsic factor) is a mouse gene.

<u>Capitalization:</u>

Rule 61. Fundamental Capitalization Rules
A proper noun is the official and complete name of a specific person, place, or thing. Capitalize a proper noun or an adjective derived from a proper noun. Avoid capitalizing a short form. A short form may be capitalized when it represents the official and complete name and distinction or emphasis is needed.

Person:
Capitalize a person's name and initials.

- Ward Stone Ireland
- J. R. R. Tolkien
  - Use a period and a space after an initial unless the name is only initials (JFK, LBJ). AP uses no space after the period (J.R.R. Tolkien).
- William Shakespeare
- Napoleon Bonaparte

For a participle in a name (de, d', de la, von), follow the source's capitalization or a biographical dictionary. A participle in a French, Spanish, or German name is frequently lowercase.

Jean d'Alembert	French
Jean de La Fontaine	French
Manuel de Falla	Spanish
Manuel de Las Casas	Spanish
Ludwig von Humboldt	German
Johannes van Keere	Dutch
Luca Da Ponte	Italian
Tawfiq al-Hakim	Arabic
Mao Tse-tung	Chinese
Kim Jung-hee	Korean

Place:
Capitalize the official and complete name of a specific place: continent, island, mountain, ocean, lake, river, world region, political division (country, state, county, ward, precinct), city, town, building, structure, monument, park, public area, street, and so on.

- Rocky Mountains; the Rockies
- Atlantic Ocean
- Mississippi River
- Australia; Down Under
- Japan
- New York City; the Big Apple
- Golden Gate Bridge
- Leaning Tower of Pisa

Thing:
Capitalize the official and complete name of a specific thing.

- Constitution of the United States; the Constitution
- The London Underground; the Underground; the Tube
- *The Age of Reason* by Thomas Paine
- The Enlightenment
- Microsoft Excel

Adjective Derived from a Proper Noun:
- Shakespearean sonnet
- Japanese dumplings
- The Napoleonic Wars

Rule 62. Title with a Person's Name

Capitalize a title before a person's name. In general, do not capitalize a title after a person's name or a title that replaces a person's name.

Title Before a Person's Name:
Always capitalized a title before a person's name.

- In 1992, Major John Smith led troops into combat.
- Did Mayor Margaret Clark speak at the fundraiser?

Title Replaces or Is After a Person's Name:
In formal writing, do not capitalize a title after a person's name or a title that replaces a person's name.

- Did Margaret Clark, mayor of the City of Menlo Park, speak at the fundraiser?
- I met Dianne Feinstein, senator from California, at a campaign rally.
- The queen visited Cambridge last Thursday.

However, a title after a person's name is frequently capitalized in a promotional or ceremonial document. Also, an organization normally capitalizes a title after a person's name when the title is related to the organization.

- Margaret Clark, Mayor of the City of Menlo Park, will speak at Saturday's fundraiser.
  - In a promotional document by the fundraiser.
- Dianne Feinstein, Senator from California, made a surprise visit to the Syracuse campaign rally.
  - In a New York State Democratic Party newsletter.

Family Title:
Capitalize a family title that precedes or replaces a person's name. Do not capitalize a family title when it is preceded by a possessive pronoun (my, your, his, her, our, their).

- My brother drove Mom to the dentist appointment.
- Did Aunt Julia drive my nephew to see a doctor.

Direct Address:
Capitalize a title without a surname in direct address. Use commas to separate direct address (Rule 14).

- Is it true that you stole city funds, Mayor?
- What time, Sargent, did you arrive at the accident?

Rule 63. North, South, East, and West

Capitalize *north, south, east, west, northeast,* and so on when it refers to a specific geographical area. Do not capitalize these words when they refer to direction or a general location.

- I moved from the East Coast to the South in 2018.
- Mrs. Anderson is a respected lawyer in the Midwest.
- The car traveled north on Michigan Street.
- My office is about thirty minutes northeast of my home.
- How many Amish communities are in northern Ohio?

Rule 64. Title or Subtitle

Capitalize the title and subtitle of a published, produced, or released work. Capitalize the title of a heading, table, chart, graph, figure, or diagram within a work.

Capitalize the first and last word and all words except
- articles (a, an, the).
- coordinating conjunctions (and, but, or, for, nor, so, yet).
- all prepositions, except when used adjectivally or adverbially (Hit the On Button, Turn Up the Volume).
- the word *to* in an infinitive (Nothing to See).

CMOS and MLA follow the above rule for prepositions. APA capitalizes all prepositions, except short prepositions of three or fewer letters. GRM and AP capitalize all prepositions, except short prepositions unless used adjectivally or adverbially. AP capitalizes *to* in an infinitive.

For a hyphenated word, follow the above rules and capitalize as if the word was not hyphenated.
- Marriage in the Middle Ages: A Comprehensive Guide
- How to Buy the Best Real Estate without Any Cash.
  - GRM, AP, and APA would capitalize *without*.
- The Gentle Art of Forgiving and Forgetting
- How to Live Life with Both Feet off the Floor
- Sit Down and Listen: From On Button to Off Button
- A Review of Up-to-Date Computer Systems

See Rule 58 for using italics with a title.

Rule 65. Organization, Business, or Government Body
Capitalize the official and complete name of an organization, association, foundation, institution, club, union, society, political party, company, business, university, college, school, or government body. Capitalize the official and complete name of any subdivision (board, committee, department, division), meeting, or conference.

In general, do not capitalize a short form of the official name. A short form may be capitalized (1) when it represents the official name and distinction or emphasis is needed or (2) when it is contained in documents or promotional literature produced by the organization, business, or government body.

The short form of a national-level judicial, legislative, or administrative body is often capitalized (Supreme Court, Congress, House, Senate, Parliament, the Treasury).

Do not capitalize the generic use of *board, city, committee, company, council, county, court, department, federal, government, state*, or *union*.

Organization or Business:
- The National Shorthand Reporters Association was founded in 1899. The association changed its name to the Nation Court Reporters Association in 1990.
  - In the second sentence, *association* may be capitalized in a document by the organization.
- My mother is a Democrat; my father is a Republican.
  - Capitalize members of a political party.
- Headquartered in Cupertino, California, Apple was founded in 1976 as Apple Computer Company.
  - Apple is the common name for Apple Inc., the company's official name since 2007.

Government Body:
- The Clark County Board of Supervisors meets Tuesdays and Wednesdays. The board meets Thursdays in a closed session for confidential matters.
  - In the second sentence, *board* may be capitalized in a document by Clark County.
- The gallery is open whenever the Senate is in session.
- The City of New York prohibits the sale of fireworks.
- The city prohibits the sale of fireworks.
  - In a city document, *city* may be capitalized.
- The federal government is corrupt.

Rule 66. Brand, Trademark, Product, or Software Name
Capitalize a brand, product, trademark, or software name. If the name refers to the product in general, do not capitalize it. Consult a dictionary.

- Can you use Microsoft Excel and Google Earth?
- Because flu season is approaching, stock up on Robitussin, Tylenol, and Sudafed.
- Do you have a thermos or Crest toothpaste? Yes, it is in my Ford truck.
  - *Thermos*, a brand name, is now a common term.

Rule 67. Days, Months, Holidays, or Seasons

Capitalize the name of a holiday, religious day, day of the week, month of the year, or any officially designated day. Do not capitalize season names.

- Is the staff meeting on Wednesday or Thursday?
- William always confuses Memorial Day, which is in May, with Labor Day, which comes in September.
- Never move to Phoenix in the middle of summer.

Holidays, Religious Days, and Designated Days Include:

April Fools' Day	Guy Fawkes Day	New Year's Eve
Ash Wednesday	Halloween	Palm Sunday
Ashura	Hanukkah	Passover
Boxing Day	Independence Day	Presidents' Day
Christmas Day	Juneteenth	Queen's Birthday
Christmas Eve	Kwanzaa	Ramadan
Cinco de Mayo	Labor Day	Remembrance Day
Columbus Day	Lent	Rosh Hashanah
Earth Day	Lincoln's Birthday	St. Patrick's Day
Easter Sunday	Martin Luther King	Thanksgiving Day
Election Day	Jr. Day	Valentine's Day
Father's Day	Mawlid	Veterans Day
Flag Day	Memorial Day	Washington's
Fourth of July	Mother's Day	Birthday
Good Friday	New Year's Day	Yom Kippur
Groundhog Day		

Rule 68. Ethnic Groups, Nationalities, and Languages

Capitalize the name of an ethnic group, racial group, nationality, or language.

- When was the first contact between Italians and the Chinese?
- Sandy described the thief as "a short Caucasian man speaking broken English."
- Franco said his new girlfriend is Asian American and speaks fluent Mandarin Chinese.
  - Write a compound nationality as an open compound.

A term used for an ethnic or racial group may change with time or may reflect a personal preference. Terms include African American, Asian, Asian American, European American, Native American, Black, White, Hispanic, Latino, Latina, Latinx, and so on. For current usage of ethnic and racial terms, consult the APA's "Racial and Ethnic Identity" (Section 5.7) or the AP's "Race-Related Coverage."

Rule 69. Laws, Historical Events, or Government Programs
Capitalize the name of a law or act; government program; or historical age, event, or program.

- The Americans with Disabilities Act (ADA) prohibits discrimination based on disability.
- Counterfeiting was an effective war tactic during the Revolutionary War.
- Thomas Paine wrote *The Age of Reason* during the Enlightenment in the late eighteenth century.
  - Do not capitalize decades or centuries.
- The New Deal focused on relief, recovery, and reform.

Rule 70. Scientific and Medical Terms
Capitalize the name of a celestial body, an official geologic term, or the Latin name of a plant or animal. For a medical term (disease, treatment, anatomical part), only capitalize a proper name or proper adjective in the term.

- The Crab Nebula is in the Perseus Arm of the Milky Way.
- The Pleistocene epoch ended about 12,000 years ago.
- Alfred identified the plant as deergrass (*Trichophorum cespitosum*)
- The biopsy was negative for non-Hodgkin's lymphoma.
- The Eustachian tube is better known as the auditory tube.

Plant and Animal Names:
Consult a dictionary. Generally, capitalize the Latin name of a plant or animal, and italicize the name of the species and subspecies (Rule 60). CMOS recommends only capitalizing a proper name or proper adjective in a common name.

Earth, Sun, and Moon:
Do not capitalize *earth, sun,* or *moon* in nontechnical writing.
Technical use often occurs with other planets in the context.
- Julia has a down to earth personality.
- Both Earth and Mars have an atmosphere.

Medical Terms:
Consult a medical dictionary for the spelling and capitalization of a medical term: a disease, infection, disorder, therapy, treatment, procedure, or anatomical part. CMOS and APA recommend only capitalizing a proper name or proper adjective in a medical term.

Rule 71. Religious Terms

Capitalize the name of a religion, religious movement, religious adherent, or an adjective derived therefrom. Capitalize a reference to a supreme being, religious building, religious event (past or future), or a work regarded as sacred. Major theological concepts are often capitalized.

- Do you believe in God or Allah as contained in the Bible or Qur'an?
- Born in Utah, I was raised among Mormons and Christians.
- The Church of the Nativity is a Catholic church.
- We do not know the population of Egypt at the time of the biblical Exodus.

According to the MW Dictionary, the Muslim sacred work may be spelled Koran, Quran, or Qur'an. CMOS has Koran or Qur'an. AP has Quran (preferred spelling) or Koran.

Rule 72. Military Terms

Capitalize the name of a military force (army, navy, air force), company, squadron, battalion, regiment, fleet, and so on. Capitalize the name of a war, battle, or campaign. Capitalize the name of a military (or civilian) ship, train, automobile, aircraft, or spacecraft. Italicize ship names.

CMOS italicizes ship names. MLA italicizes ship, aircraft, and spacecraft names. GRM only italicizes ship, aircraft, or spacecraft names for "special display." CMOS, GRM, and AP use the pronoun *it*, not *she*, with a ship.

- The Continental Army and the Continental Navy were founded in 1775.
- In World War II, the Allies chiefly consisted of Great Britain, the United States, and the Soviet Union.
- Andrew Jackson commanded the United States Army at the Battle of New Orleans during the War of 1812.
- The *USS Enterprise* (CVN-65) is the most decorated ship in U.S. naval history.
- Most people can recognize the Boeing B-17 Flying Fortress used during World War II.
  - MLA would italicize *B-17 Flying Fortress*.

Number Formatting:

Rule 73. Word Style and Figure Style
Popular style guides recommend either a Word Style or a Figure Style for number formatting. Formal writing mostly follows Word Style (CMOS and MLA). Journalism, business, and technical writing mainly follow Figure Style (AP, GRM, and APA).

Word Style:
Spell out a number that can be written in one or two words, counting a hyphenated word (twenty-one) as one word. Therefore, spell out one to one hundred plus some round numbers over one hundred (two hundred, five thousand).

Use figures for a number that cannot be written in one or two words. Exceptions include using figures to express a date, time, monetary amount, address, technical measurement, decimal fraction, percentage, or an ordinal (see Rules 74 to 90).

Figure Style:
Spell out a single-digit number (one to nine), and use figures for ten and above. Exceptions include using figures to express a date, time, monetary amount, address, technical measurement, decimal fraction, percentage, or an ordinal (see Rules 74 to 90).

When spelling out a number from twenty-one to ninety-nine, use a hyphen. Do not use a hyphen to spell out the portion over one hundred.

twenty-one   thirty-seven
seventy-eight   ninety-nine
five hundred   three thousand

Use a comma to separate thousands, millions, billions, and so on. Do not use a comma separator with a year, page number, line number, address number, ZIP code, telephone number, serial or invoice number, room number, or an acoustic or broadcast frequency (2000 Hz).

- The population was 987 in 1732; it grew to 25,304 in 1832; and it exploded to 1,415,439 in 1932.
- Sophia's statement that she left the company in 2015 is found on transcript page 1024.
- Nick lives at 9112 Plymouth Avenue.

Rule 74. Consistent Format for Related Numbers

Use a consistent format for related numbers in the same sentence or context. Use figures for related numbers when one number would be spelled out and another number would be expressed in figures.

- I own **forty-two** horses, and they eat about **175** bales of hay each week.
  - Word Style; numbers not related.
- I own **3** chickens and **12** dogs.
  - Figure Style; numbers related.
- I ordered **15** Christmas gifts in the morning. Later that evening, I ordered **6** more gifts.
  - Figure Style; numbers related.

Rule 75. Number in Millions, Billions, or Trillions

When a number or monetary amount is in the millions, billions, or trillions, use figures with the word *million, billion,* or *trillion.* The figure must be a whole number (1 million) or a whole number with only one decimal place (1.2 million). Use a consistent format in the sentence or context.

- The viral YouTube video had 1.3 million views in a single week.
- The worldwide human population is 7.7 billion.
- The U.S. national debt is $28 trillion.
- The company's revenue is $1.3 million.
- The 2016 labor cost was $950,000. In 2017 it was $1,200,000.
  - Do not format as $950,000 and $1.2 million because a consistent format is required.

AP allows up to two decimal places (1.45 million). However, a whole number or a whole number with only one decimal place dominate AP examples. It also allows the use of M for million (1.4M Without Power) and B for billion ($2B Deficit) in headlines. In informal writing or where space is limited (table, chart, graph), using K for thousand, M for million, and B for billion is acceptable.

Rule 76. Number at the Beginning of a Sentence or Title
Spell out a number at the beginning of a sentence or title. Avoid beginning a sentence or title with a number, especially when the number is expressed in more than two words, by rewriting.

- Twenty-seven cows escaped through a hole in the fence.
  - Rewrite (Word Style): In all, twenty-seven cows escaped through a hole in the fence.
  - Rewrite (Figure Style): In all, 27 cows escaped through a hole in the fence
- Three thousand people signed the pledge.
  - Rewrite (Word Style): The pledge was signed by three thousand people.
  - Rewrite (Figure Style): The pledge was signed by 3,000 people.
- One hundred twenty of the 151 applicants had work experience.
  - Rewrite (Word and Figure Style): Of the 151 applicants, 120 had work experience.

Rule 77. Dates
Use figures to express the year and the day of the month in a
date. Do not abbreviate the name of the month or the day of
the week. See examples for comma placement.

Format: *Month Day, Year*
Place a comma after the day of the month and after the year if
midsentence.
- My son was born on April 5, 2003.
- I went on June 18, 2018, to see the doctor.

Format: *DayOfWeek, Month Day, Year*
Place a comma after the day of the week, after the day of the
month, and after the year if midsentence.
- My son was born on Saturday, April 5, 2003.
- I went on Monday, June 18, 2018, to see the doctor.

Format: *Day Month Year*
No comma between date elements.
- My son was born on 5 April 2003.
- I went on 18 June 2018 to see the doctor.

Format: *Month Year*
No comma between the month and year.
- My son was born in April 2003.
- I went in June 2018 to see the doctor.

Format: *Month Day*
No comma between the month and day of the month.
- My son was born on April 5.
- I went on June 18 to see the doctor.

All-Figure Date:
In informal writing or where space is limited, all date elements
may be expressed with figures in a Month-Day-Year format
separated with slashes, periods, or hyphens. Slashes are
typical. Because this format may be confused with the Day-
Month-Year format used outside the United States, consider
abbreviating the month instead of using figures.
- My son was born on 4/5/2003.
- I went on 6-18-2018 to see the doctor.

Abbreviations:

In informal writing or where space is limited, the month or day of the week may be abbreviated. Use a three-letter abbreviation without a period.

January	Jan	Monday	Mon
February	Feb	Tuesday	Tue
March	Mar	Wednesday	Wed
April	Apr	Thursday	Thu
May	May	Friday	Fri
June	Jun	Saturday	Sat
July	Jul	Sunday	Sun
August	Aug		
September	Sep		
October	Oct		
November	Nov		
December	Dec		

Rule 78. Time

Use figures to express time before *a.m.* or *p.m.,* and place a colon between the hour and minutes. Use *noon* and *midnight* to avoid confusion with 12:00 a.m. and 12:00 p.m.

- I leave for work at 7:30 a.m. I arrive home at 5:15 p.m.
- Debbie gets up at 4:45 a.m.
- Robert normally takes lunch at noon.

In Word Style, times on the hour, half hour, and quarter hour are spelled out unless emphasis is needed.
- I leave for work at seven thirty.
- Cecilia arrived for dinner at a quarter past five.

A.M./P.M.:
Use lowercase with periods: *a.m.* or *p.m.*

AP and MLA use lowercase with periods. CMOS and GRM recommend lowercase with periods. However, both allow small capital letters: GRM with periods (A.M.) and CMOS with or without periods (A.M. or AM). The MW Dictionary lists lowercase with periods or capital letters without periods (a.m. or AM).

Time on the Hour:
Word Style includes the zeros for a time on the hour in a.m./p.m. format (7:00 a.m.). Figure Style, however, does not include the zeros (7 a.m.) unless emphasis is needed or a consistent format is required (list, table, sentence).

O'clock:
Word Style spells out the number before *o'clock*. Figure Style uses a figure before *o'clock*.

- Word Style: The meeting starts at five o'clock.
- Figure Style: The meeting starts at 5 o'clock.

24-Hour Time:
Express time in a 24-hour time format as a four-digit number with or without a colon between the hour and minutes (1315 or 13:15). Use a consistent format throughout the document, and use a colon in an unclear context.

To convert an a.m. time to 24-hour time, use the a.m. time (except with 12 use 00). To convert a p.m. time to 24-hour time, add 12 to the p.m. time (except with 12 use 12).

- 12:09 a.m. in 24-hour time is 0009 or 00:09
- 8:15 a.m. in 24-hour time is 0815 or 08:15
- 11:37 a.m. in 24-hour time is 1137 or 11:37
- 12:09 p.m. in 24-hour time is 1209 or 12:09
- 8:15 p.m. in 24-hour time is 2015 or 20:15

Rule 79. Money
Express a monetary amount with a dollar symbol ($) and figures. For an amount under one dollar, use figures with *cents*.

- My rent is $1,800 per month.
- The dress listed online from $100 to $125.
- The wholesale cost for the stationery is $1.43.
- That large can of tomato sauce is only 79 cents.

In Word Style, spell out isolated monetary amounts that can be written in one or two words plus *dollars* or *cents* (thirty-five cents, nineteen dollars, three thousand dollars).

Amount under One Dollar:
For an amount under one dollar, use figures with *cents* (35 cents) unless a consistent format requires a decimal amount ($0.35). Use a zero before the decimal point.

- For 75 cents, you can purchase the newspaper.
- A head of lettuce is $1.95, and a large onion is $0.65.

Even Monetary Amount:
For an even monetary amount ($5), the decimal point and zeros are <u>not</u> required ($5.00) unless emphasis is needed or a consistent format is required (list, table, sentence).

- The dress ranged online from $100 to $125.
- Can you believe I found this belt for exactly $15.00?
  - Zeros used for emphasis.
- The pack of brushes is $9.00, or each brush is $0.95.
  - Zeros used for consistency.

Foreign Monetary Amount:
Format a foreign monetary amount like a U.S. monetary amount. Before the amount, place the three-letter currency code with one space or the currency symbol with no space.

- A train ticket to Berlin costs EUR 40 (or €40).
- How much is MXN 200 in U.S. dollars?
  - MXN means Mexican peso.

Rule 80. Addresses
Use figures to express the address number and ZIP code. For a numbered street, spell out first to ninth and use figures for above ninth (Third Avenue, 10th Street). Do not abbreviate the state or street name (Arkansas, Illinois, Avenue, Drive).

CMOS spells out numbered streets from first to hundredth. GRM recommends using *One* instead of 1 for an address number to improve clarity (One Main Street).

- I live at 4550 Live Oak Way.
- I live at 914 Third Avenue.
- I live at 6109 44th Avenue.
  - CMOS: I live at 6109 Forty-Fourth Avenue.

Address (Envelope Format):
Place the address number and street name on the first line without a comma between them. Any apartment number or room number follows on the first line separated with a comma. Place the city, state, and ZIP code on the second line. Place a comma only between the city and state.

> 914 Third Street
> Kirtland, Ohio 44024
>
> 220 Cornwall Road, Apartment 42
> Woodside, California 94062

Address (Sentence Format):
Use "Envelope Format" with a comma instead of the line break. Place a comma after the ZIP code if the address is midsentence.

- My address is 914 Third Street, Kirtland, Ohio 44024.
- Please use 220 Cornwall Road, Apartment 42, Woodside, California 94062, for all correspondence.

Address (Sentence Format with Omitted Information):
Use "Sentence Format" for the included address information.

- I live on Third Street, Kirtland, Ohio.
- Use my address in Woodside, California, for all correspondence.
  - Comma after *California* because the address is midsentence.

Street Abbreviations:
Do not abbreviate the street name in formal writing unless it is contained in a list, table, or bibliography. AP abbreviates a street name when the address number is included (1600 Pennsylvania Ave.). An abbreviation on a mailing envelope is acceptable.

Street Name	Abbrev.	Street Name	Abbrev.
Avenue	Ave.	Lane	Ln.
Boulevard	Blvd.	Parkway	Pkwy.
Court	Ct.	Place	Pl.
Drive	Dr.	Post Office Box	P.O. Box
Expressway	Expy.	Road	Rd.
Highway	Hwy.	Street	St.

Do not abbreviate *North, East, South*, or *West* in a street name unless contained in a list, table, or bibliography. AP abbreviates these words when the address number is included (562 W. 43rd St.). An abbreviation on a mailing envelope is acceptable.

North	N.	South	S.
East	E.	West	W.

U.S. State Abbreviations:

Do not abbreviate the state name in formal writing unless contained in a list, table, or bibliography. AP abbreviates the state name in a complete address (914 Third Street, Kirtland, OH 44024). Use an abbreviation on a mailing envelope.

State	Abbrev.	State	Abbrev.
Alabama	AL	Nebraska	NE
Alaska	AK	Nevada	NV
Arizona	AZ	New Hampshire	NH
Arkansas	AR	New Jersey	NJ
California	CA	New Mexico	NM
Colorado	CO	New York	NY
Connecticut	CT	North Carolina	NC
Delaware	DE	North Dakota	ND
Florida	FL	Ohio	OH
Georgia	GA	Oklahoma	OK
Hawaii	HI	Oregon	OR
Idaho	ID	Pennsylvania	PA
Illinois	IL	Rhode Island	RI
Indiana	IN	South Carolina	SC
Iowa	IA	South Dakota	SD
Kansas	KS	Tennessee	TN
Kentucky	KY	Texas	TX
Louisiana	LA	Utah	UT
Maine	ME	Vermont	VT
Maryland	MD	Virginia	VA
Massachusetts	MA	Washington	WA
Michigan	MI	Washington, DC	DC
Minnesota	MN	West Virginia	WV
Mississippi	MS	Wisconsin	WI
Missouri	MO	Wyoming	WY
Montana	MT		

Rule 81. Technical Measurement
Use figures to express a technical measurement, such as length, width, area, weight, volume, distance, time, or temperature. Do not separate parts of a measurement with punctuation (6 feet 2 inches). Repeat the symbol with a number range (10°C–20°C), but use the measurement word or abbreviation only with the last number (8 by 10 feet).

- Ethan timed his drive to Los Angeles: 8 hours.
- Clara is 12 years 8 months.
- The hole measured 3 by 5 inches.
- The freezer operates between 30°F–36°F.

CMOS expresses any technical measurement using a symbol or abbreviation in figures.

Abbreviations:
Only use an abbreviation in technical writing or where space is limited (table, chart, graph). Common abbreviations include the following:

degree Fahrenheit	°F	centimeter	cm
feet, foot	ft	cubic centimeter	cc
gallon	gal	degree Celsius	°C
inch	in	gram	gm
mile	mi	kilogram	kg
miles per hour	mph	liter	L
ounce	oz	meter	m
pound	lb	millimeter	mm
yard	yd	milliliter	ml
hour	hr	cubic	cu
minute	min	parts per million	ppm
second	s	pounds per square inch	psi

In very technical writing, a prime replaces *feet* (8 feet is 8'), and a double prime replaces *inches* (5 inches is 5"). An *x* may replace the word *by*.

- The hole measured 3" x 5".
  - 3 inches by 5 inches.
- My living room is 12' x 14'.
  - 12 feet by 14 feet.

Rule 82. Decimal Fraction

Use figures to express a decimal fraction (8.5). Use a zero before the decimal point for an amount less than one (0.5). However, do not use a zero before the decimal point when the number cannot be greater than one: gun caliber, batting average, and some statistical values.

- At the last weight-loss meeting, I lost 2.3 pounds.
- The instructions are in boldface—slowly add 0.35 grams of magnesium.
- We found the murder weapon: a Colt .45 handgun.

Rule 83. Percentage

In business or nontechnical writing, use figures with *percent* to express a percentage. In journalism, technical writing, or where space is limited (table, chart, graph) use figures with a percent symbol (%) to express a percentage. Repeat the symbol with a number range (15%–20%), and use a zero before the decimal point for a percentage less than one (0.5%).

Business or Nontechnical Writing:
- Students averaged 82 percent on the midterm.
- The inflation rate in 2017 was 3.2 percent.
- Annual growth rates varied between 0.2 and 4.7 percent.

Journalism or Technical Writing:
- Students averaged 82% on the midterm.
- The inflation rate in 2017 was 3.2%.
- Annual growth rates varied between 0.2% and 4.7%.

Rule 84. Fractions

Use words to express a fraction unless it exceeds two words, is a mixed number, or is a technical measurement. A hyphenated word counts as one word.

Hyphenate a fraction unless the second element is already hyphenated (two-thirds, nine-sixteenths, one twenty-fifth).

Use a "self-made" fraction when the fraction is more than two words (21/25) or is a technical measurement (3/4 inch). Use figures and a slash (/) with no space before and after the slash. A "ready-made" fraction may be used (¾ inch), but use a consistent format within the context.

- We need a two-thirds majority for approval.
- I never let my gas tank drop below one-half.
- Is seven-sixteenths of the U.S. population obese?
- The annual report showed 27/64 of the company's profit went to executive bonuses.
  - Fraction is more than two words.
- The depth of the crack is 5/16 of an inch.
  - Fraction is a technical measurement.

Use figures plus a "self-made" fraction to create a mixed number (3 1/4). Insert one space between the whole number and the fraction. Do not use a hyphen. A ready-made fraction may be used, but do not insert a space between the whole number and the fraction (3¼). Use a consistent format within the context.

- Her child is 4 1/2 months old.
- Her child is 4½ months old.

Rule 85. Ordinals
Word Style spells out ordinals from first to hundredth and uses figures above one hundredth (101st). Figure Style spells out ordinals from first to ninth and uses figures above ninth (10th). Only use superscript *st, nd, rd,* and *th* in informal writing.

CMOS follows Word Style, AP and MLA follow Figure Style. GRM follows Word Style but allows Figure Style for emphasis. APA allows either style as long as consistency is maintained.

- Isabella won second place at the spelling bee.
- Word Style: Her brother finished twelfth in the race.
- Figure Style: Her brother finished 12th in the race.
- As a novice runner, Chris placed 110th in the marathon.

See Rule 80 for numbered streets.

Rule 86. Inclusive Numbers
Use an en dash (–) between two numbers to show a range. A hyphen is used in journalism, MLA style, informal writing, or when the en dash is not available. Do not use an en dash when the words *from* or *between* introduce the number range.

- The cost analysis is on pages 158–165.
- During 2015–2017, the department had a budget surplus.
- A severe drought occurred between 1928 and 1935.

When a range of pages or years occurs frequently in the document, abbreviate the second number using the following guidelines. Do not abbreviate infrequent or isolated ranges.

1. Do not abbreviate if the first number is under 100.
   9–16   49–53
2. Do not abbreviate if the first number is a multiple of 100.
   100–107   1200–1217
3. The abbreviation is the changed numbers in the second number. Use at least a two-digit abbreviation unless the leading digit of the abbreviation is a zero.

Range	Abbreviation
1997–2003	None
1493–1502	1493–502
134–138	134–38
258–277	258–77
1997–1998	1997–98
102–108	102–8

4. A slash may be used between consecutive years to indicate the last part of the first year and the first part of the second year.
   1997/98   2018/19

Rule 87. Adjacent Numbers
When two adjacent numbers are both expressed in words or figures, separated them with a comma.

When two adjacent numbers are part of a compound modifier, use words for one number and use figures for the other number. Generally, use words for the first number unless the second number would be much shorter if expressed in words.

Both Numbers Expressed in Words or Numbers:
- In 2017 nine students failed the final exam.
  - No comma necessary because both numbers are not expressed in words or figures.
- In 2017, 52 students failed the final exam.
- For the staff meeting at five, ten people will attend.
- For Account 933216, $342.75 was charged on March 9.
  - Comma also required per Rule 5.

Compound Modifier:
- Maggie owns two 6-room homes.
- Liam received twelve $50 gift cards for his birthday.
- Kaitlyn found 150 twenty-dollar bills in a paper bag.
- Aidan needs 525 two-page leaflets printed.

Rule 88. Plural of a Number
Form the plural of a number by adding *s*.

- Tonight's low temperature will be in the 20s.
- Computer proliferation exploded in the 1980s.
- Madison's ZIP code contains two 5s.

Rule 89. Numbered References
Express a numbered reference as a figure. Most reference words in journalism, business writing, and technical writing are capitalized. In formal writing, the reference word is lowercase. Separate numbered references with a comma.

Examples Using Business Style (GRM) Capitalization:
- I love Act 2, Scene 7, of Shakespeare's *As You Like It*.
- Mr. Smith's testimony starts on page 5, line 10, of the deposition dated September 19, 2019.
- The ordinance language the council member quoted is Chapter 1, Section 108, paragraph 3.
- Whose name is on Policy No. 2304997?

Abbreviate *number* as *No.* and *numbers* as *Nos.* when used between the reference word and figure. Formal writing prefers lowercase (no. and nos.). Using *No.* is often unnecessary (Invoice 20934, Question 39, Room 7).

Capitalization of the Reference Word:
Journalism, business writing, and technical writing normally capitalize the reference word. Conversely, formal writing uses lowercase.

	Capitalized Words	Lowercase Words
CMOS/MLA	None	All words
AP	All words except "Lowercase Words"	*line* and *size*
GRM	All words except "Lowercase Words"	*page, paragraph, sentence, line, verse, note, size*, and *step*
APA	All words except "Lowercase Words"	*page* and *paragraph*

Rule 90. Ratios, Scores, Voting Results, and Mathematics
Use figures to express a number in a ratio, proportion, betting odd, voting result, sports score or standing, or mathematical expression. Use a hyphen as shown in the examples.

Note the two common formats in the below examples (using 8 and 1): "a ratio of 8 to 1" and an "8-to-1 ratio." AP uses an abbreviated format with only a hyphen (an 8-1 ratio). The word *ratio* could be replaced with *majority* (a ratio), *odds, chance* (an odd), *vote*, and so on.

- A ratio of 5 to 2. (AP: 5-to-2)
- A 5-to-2 ratio. (AP: 5-2)
    - Technical writing allows: A 5:2 ratio.
- A proportion of powder and water of 1 to 3.
- Use 1 part powder to 3 parts water.
- The odds were 100 to 1. (AP: 100-1)
- A 100-to-1 chance. (AP: 100-1)
- A vote of 18 to 9. (AP: 18-9)
- An 18-to-9 vote. (AP & GRM: 18-9)
- The team lost 4 to 3. (AP: 4-3)
- The team now has a 12-4-2 record.
- Multiply by 7 and divide by 2.

<u>Abbreviations:</u>

Rule 91. Abbreviations

Use abbreviations sparingly. In formal writing, reserve abbreviations for tables, source citations, parenthetical notes, and bibliographies. In business writing, limit abbreviations to emails, memos, forms, catalogs, and internal letters. In technical writing for science and technology, however, abbreviations occur frequently.

- The ATM had no money to withdraw.
- The appointment is with Dr. Anna Wells at 3 p.m.
- Alexander III of Macedon, better known as Alexander the Great, died in 323 BC.
- The Federal Highway Administration (FHWA) released the latest accident data on Friday.

Some abbreviations are always acceptable: *Dr., Mr., Mrs., Ms., Mx., Jr., Sr.,* a.m., p.m., BC, and AD.

Capitalized abbreviations typically have no spaces or periods (AIDS, ATM, IBM), and lowercase abbreviations normally have no spaces with periods (a.k.a., a.m., vol.). An abbreviation with an ampersand has no spaces (R&D).

Defining an Abbreviation:
Do not define common abbreviations (p.m., ATM, GPS). Define uncommon abbreviations, author-created abbreviations, and abbreviations unfamiliar to the audience.

Do not define an abbreviation for an infrequently used term—fewer than three times within a chapter or article. Avoid defining too many abbreviations, but when many abbreviations are necessary, provide a list of abbreviations.

To define an abbreviation, write out the full term with the first occurrence followed by the abbreviation in parentheses. Use only the abbreviation thereafter. Do not mix writing out the full term and using the abbreviation. However, an abbreviation not used for a long time may be redefined.

Rule 92. Common Abbreviations

The use of certain abbreviations is always acceptable (see below). Other abbreviations are best reserved for specific fields.

Abbreviations That Are Always Acceptable:
Using the following abbreviations is always acceptable:

- Before a name: *Dr., Mr., Mrs., Ms.,* or *Mx.*
- After a name: *Jr.* or *Sr.*
- After a year: *BC, AD, BCE,* or *CE.*
- After a time: *a.m.* or *p.m.*

BCE and CE, instead of BC and AD, are widely used in academic fields, especially archeology, history, and theology. AP and GRM use periods (B.C. and A.D.). Other popular style guides and the MW Dictionary do not use periods (BC and AD).

Common Business Abbreviations:

a.k.a.	also known as	LLP	limited liability partnership
AP	accounts payable	misc.	miscellaneous
ASAP	as soon as possible	NA	not applicable/available
c/o	care of	OTC	over the counter
Co.	company	pd.	paid
Corp.	corporation	POS	point of sale/service
CPI	consumer price index	Q&A	question and answer
CPM	cost per thousand	QA	quality assurance
d/b/a	doing business as	QC	quality control
FY	fiscal year	ROI	return on investment
GL	general ledger	SSN	social security number
LLC	limited liability company	TBD	to be determined

Common Academic Abbreviations:

b.	born	no.	number
ca.	*circa,* about	p.	page (pp. for pages)
ch.	chapter	par.	paragraph
d.	died	qtd.	quoted in
dept.	department	s.v.	under the word
ed.	editor, edition	sec.	section
ff.	and following	trans.	translated by
fig.	figure	U	University
ibid.	in the same place	UP	University Press
MS	manuscript	v.	verse (vv. for verses)
n.d.	no date	vol.	volume
n.p.	no publisher/page	yr.	year

Abbreviate *United States* as US or U.S. Both CMOS and MLA use US; GRM and APA use U.S.; AP uses U.S. in articles and US in headlines. MW Dictionary lists US or U.S. as acceptable.

Common Latin Abbreviations:
Avoid using Latin abbreviations in the running text. They are more appropriate for source citations or parenthetical notes.

Latin Abbreviation	Running Text Substitute
cf. (*confer*)	compare
e.g. (*exempli gratia*)	for example, such as
etc. (*et cetera*)	and so on, and so forth
i.e. (*id est*)	that is

See Rule 75 for large number abbreviations.

See Rule 77 for month and day of the week abbreviations.

See Rule 80 for address and state abbreviations.

See Rule 81 for technical measurement abbreviations.

Rule 93. Professional Degree or Title after a Person's Name

Do not use periods in a professional degree or title following a person's name.

- Rebecca Farley, DDS, extracted the tooth.
- We spoke to Mr. Smith, PhD, for more information.
- Michelle Wu, PE, is an expert in suspension bridges.

AP uses periods; therefore, the above examples would use D.D.S., Ph.D., and P.E.

Rule 94. Plural of an Abbreviation

Form the plural of a capitalized abbreviation by adding *s*. Form the plural of a lowercase abbreviation by adding an apostrophe and *s*.

- Pat sold three TVs today.
- How many IOUs before a person says enough?
- The software blocked two suspicious URLs.
- The email had eight cc's.

<u>Lists:</u>

A vertical list highlights each point. The vertical format emphasizes the text, increasing clarity because each item is separated instead of being locked in a block of words. The list format also helps readers remember key points and make connections to related points.

A vertical list is ordered or unordered. A sequential number precedes each item in an ordered list. Likewise, a filled circle or square normally precedes each item in an unordered list.

Two keys to creating a well-constructed list are consistency and parallelism. Some style guides, like *The Gregg Reference Manual*, allow formatting options. Therefore, select and use a consistent format, especially for similar lists close together in the document.

Parallelism is the overlooked key to writing a good list. List items should be parallel in phrasing and formatting, having the

- same structure (complete sentence, phrase, or word).
- same sentence type (statement or question).
- same verb tense.
- same part of speech beginning each item.
- same general length for each item.

Introductory Sentence or Phrase:
A list requires an introduction expressing its purpose. According to CMOS, a complete sentence followed by a colon is the "best way" to introduce a list.

Follow an introductory phrase or sentence with a colon. Always use a colon with an introduction containing the phrase *as follows* or *the following*. However, do not use a colon when an introductory phrase is the beginning of a full sentence grammatically completed by each list item.

Ordered List:
A "numbered list" is another name for an ordered list because a number precedes each item. Use an ordered list when the items are arranged by time, priority, task order, relative importance, or textual reference (previous or subsequent).

Guidelines for formatting an ordered list:

- **Introduction**. Use an introductory phrase or sentence. Insert a space between the introduction and the ordered list. CMOS and AP do not use a space.
- **Indent**. Indent the list from the left margin.
- **Item Number**. Use a sequential number with a period before each item.
- **Parallelism**. Use consistent phrasing and formatting with all items.
- **Capitalization**. Capitalize the first word of each item.
- **End Punctuation**. Use end punctuation if the item is a complete sentence or when it forms a complete sentence with the introductory phrase.
- **Runover Alignment**. Align the text on an additional line with the above item text.
- **Extra Paragraph**. Insert a space between the item and the paragraph. Align the text with the above item text.
- **Subitems**. Format subitems like an ordered list. However, use a lowercase letter with a period for the "Item Number." Indent the subitems and align the lowercase letter with the above ordered item text.
- **Space Between Items**. While APA and MLA use a space between items, a space is usually not necessary. A space improves clarity when (1) items are two or more lines, (2) an item has an extra paragraph, or (3) an item has subitems.
- **Space After List**. Use a space after the list.

This is an example of an ordered list:

1. Use a space between the introduction and the list.
2. Each item begins with a number followed by a period.
3. When the text continues to an additional line, align the text with the above item text.
4. While APA and MLA use a space between items, a space is usually not necessary. A space improves clarity in some situations.

This is another example of an ordered list:

1. Capitalize the first word of each item.

    a. A subitem begins with a lowercase letter and a period. Format a subitem like an ordered list item.

    b. Align the lowercase letter for a subitem with the ordered item text.

2. Use consistent phrasing and formatting with all items.

    An extra paragraph is separated by a space. Align the text with the above item text.

3. A space between items is usually not necessary. The spaces in this ordered list improve the clarity of the subitems and extra paragraph.

Unordered List:
A "bulleted list" is another name for an unordered list because a symbol, normally a filled circle or square, often precedes each item. Use an unordered list when the list items are <u>not</u> arranged by time, priority, task order, relative importance, or textual reference (previous or subsequent).

Format an unordered list like an ordered list, except for the following:

*   **Item Symbol**. An unordered list often uses a symbol, a filled circle or square, before each item instead of a number. Use an asterisk (*) when traditional symbols are not available.

*   **Subitems**. Precede each unordered subitem with a symbol instead of a lowercase letter. The symbol is normally an open circle or square, matching the item symbol. Use two adjacent hyphens (--) when traditional symbols are not available. Indent subitems and align the subitem symbol with the unordered item text.

Examples of an unordered list occur throughout this section and book (see pages 12, 23, 42, 52, and 53).

A "simple" unordered list does not use a symbol before each item. Use a simple list when all or most items are written on one line—items are often a word or short phrase—and when all items contain no extra paragraphs or subitems. Format a simple unordered list like an ordered list, except for the following:

- **Item Symbol**. Symbol not used.

- **Indent**. None. Items may be arranged in two or more columns to avoid a long, narrow list.

- **Capitalization**. The first word may be capitalized or lowercase. Be consistent.

- **Runover Alignment**. Avoid runover. Indent runover unless a space is used between items.

- **Extra Paragraph**. Extra paragraphs are not allowed.

- **Subitems**. Subitems are not allowed.

- **Space Between Items**. Usually none. All or most items should be written on one line.

Examples of a simple unordered list occur throughout this book (see pages 6, 31, 33, 48, 93, 100, and 104).

Run-In List:
Use a run-in list to emphasize three or more brief items. Enclose the numbers or lowercase letters that separate the items in parentheses. Numbers are typically used unless the document is in APA style or the list is a subitem of an ordered list.

- Capitalize after a colon if (1) the word is a proper noun, (2) two or more related sentences follow, or (3) one or more sentences follow that require special emphasis.
  - APA style would use lowercase letters.

- 2. The interviewee forgot to provide the following information: (a) contact phone number, (b) copy on an academic degree, and (c) three references.
  - Run-in list is a subitem of an ordered list.

<u>Tables:</u>
A table effectively presents a large amount of data. Do not duplicate the table's data in the running text. Instead, discuss the conclusions reached by the data in the running text. Keep the following questions in mind when creating a table:

- Is the purpose of the table clear?
- Is the data presented in an easy-to-understand way?

If the answer is no to either question, then revise, simplify, or possibly remove the table.

Reference the table number, not the page number, in the running text. Then insert the table as soon as possible after the first reference. A table less than one page may be placed at the top or bottom of a page separated from the running text by two spaces.

Table 1. Table Title

| Stub column title | Spanner title[a] | | Spanner title | |
	Column title	Column title[b]	Column title	Column title
Entry	0.0	—	0.0	n.a.
Subentry	1.0	1.2	10.0	12.3
Subentry	2.0	2.3	20.0	23.4
Entry[c]	3.0	3.4	30.0	34.5
Entry	4.0[d]	4.5	40.0	45.6

Source: The data source, if not from the author, in source citation format.

Note: This note applies to the entire table. Any *Source* or *Note* runover is aligned to the left margin. Use a space after *Source* and *Note*.

[a] This note applies to all data in the columns under the spanner title.

[b] This note applies to all data under the column title. Any footnote runover is aligned to the left margin. Use a space after each footnote.

[c] This note applies to all data in the row.

[d] This note applies to one data cell.

Table Number and Title:
Number tables sequentially in order of running-text appearance (Table 1, Table 2).

Capitalize the title per Rule 64. Use a brief and unbiased description of the data: "Crime Rates of Major U.S. Cities" instead of "Alarming Crime Rate Escalation in Major U.S. Cities". A title with a noun and participle is better than a title with a noun and relative clause. "Populations Using Home Delivery" is better than "Populations That Use Home Delivery".

Column Titles:
A column title applies to one column of data, and a spanner title applies to two or more columns. The leftmost column is called the stub column.

Title. A column title must be brief, and use abbreviations as necessary (see Abbreviations). The sub column title may be omitted when the entries and subentries are clear on their own. All column titles within the table and similar tables should be parallel and consistent.

Capitalization. CMOS recommends only capitalizing the first word and words normally capitalized, like a proper noun. CMOS also allows capitalization per Rule 64. APA only capitalizes the first word and words normally capitalized. GRM capitalizes per Rule 64.

Alignment. A spanner title is centered across the columns, and a column title is typically centered. The stub column title is traditionally aligned left. For all column titles on the same horizontal row, vertically align the columns to the lowest line when column titles are two or more lines.

Stub Entries and Subentries:
Stub entries and subentries are items or grouped items in the leftmost column. Columns located right of the stub column contain data about the stub entries and subentries.

Title. A stub entry or subentry title must be brief, and use abbreviations as necessary (see Abbreviations). All stub entry titles within the table and similar tables should be parallel and consistent.

Capitalization. Capitalize the first word of an entry or subentry. Do not end an entry or subentry with a period.

Alignment. Align an entry or subentry to the left.

Runover. When a table uses a space between entries, the runover is aligned to the left margin. When no space is used between entries and the entry has no indented subentries, indent the runover the width of a capital M. If the entry has indented subentries, indent the runover the width of two capital Ms.

Subentry. Format a subentry like an entry, but indent the width of a capital M. Align any runover with the above subentry text.

Abbreviations:
Use abbreviations likely to be understood by the audience, and define any unfamiliar abbreviations in a note. In a title, enclose a unit of measure or an important clarifying word in parentheses: ($), ($M), (%), (tested), (actual). Place any detailed information in a note.

Cell Formatting:
Align the cells under a column containing data for the stub entry or subentry. Use a consistent vertical and horizontal alignment within a column.

Numbers. Do not include a unit of measure in a cell when it is specified in the column title. Center a column on the longest number. Additionally, align numbers without a decimal point on the last digit to align any comma separators. Align numbers with a decimal point on the decimal point, and use the same number of decimal places.

Words. Align runover to the left when a space is used between cells, but indent runover the width of a capital M when no space is used between cells. If no runover is present in the column, the text may be centered. A column of cells with long text might look better if aligned left. Use a consistent horizontal alignment within the column and with other similar columns in the table.

When a stub entry has more than one line of text and the cell text is only one line, align the cell text with the stub entry's bottom line. When a stub entry and the cell text both have more than one line of text, align the cell text with the stub entry's top line. Use a consistent vertical alignment within the column and with other similar columns in the table.

Empty Cell. When a cell does not apply, leave it blank. When a cell applies but has no data, place a centered em dash (—) in the cell. If an em dash is not available, use three centered periods (…). As an alternative, use the abbreviations *n/a* (not applicable) and *n.d.* (no data) with the definitions in the table note.

Table Notes:
A table note may be a source note, a general note, a footnote, or a probability note.

Spacing and Runover. Use a space between notes and footnotes. Align any runover to the left margin.

Source Note. When the table data is not from the author, cite all sources in citation format. Use "Source:" or "Sources:" in italics followed by the sources in order of appearance from top to bottom or left to right.

General Note. Notes or abbreviations applying to the entire table follow a source note. Use "Note:" in italics followed by the table-wide notes and then by abbreviation definitions.

APA Format. APA combines the source note and general note into a single note. Use "Note." in italics followed by the general note information then by the source note information.

Footnotes. A footnote may apply to a row, column, spanner, or specific cell. Use superscript letters ([a], [b], [c]) in the table and notes section to avoid confusion with any superscript numbers for running-text footnotes. Order footnotes from top to bottom then left to right. Unlike running-text footnotes, a table footnote may apply to more than one table element.

Probability Note. A probability note shows the results of statistical hypotheses testing using asterisks and other symbols, usually a dagger (†). The probability, expressed with the letter *p,* shows if the correlation between two things is meaningful or just coincidence. When the correlation has a 5 percent or less chance of being random, it is expressed as "* *p*<.05" (no zero before the decimal point). Typical probability notes are * *p*<.05, ** *p*<.01, and *** *p*<.001.

Horizontal and Vertical Lines:
Use horizontal lines sparingly. The only required horizontal lines are (1) below the table title, (2) below a spanner title, (3) below a column title, (4) above a total or subtotal, and (5) below the table and before any notes.

Avoid vertical lines to separate data. Instead, use spacing and row and column alignment to clarify the relationship of the data. Vertical lines might occur in a large table to improve clarity and comprehension.

Large Tables:
When a table is too long or too wide to fit on one page, the best practice is to simplify the table or to create separate tables.

For a table longer than one page, all subsequent pages should repeat the spanner and column titles and have the table number with *continued* at the top of the page (Table 1 Continued).

For a table wider than one page, use landscape page orientation—table text reads from page bottom to page top. If the landscape-oriented table is longer than one page, all subsequent pages should repeat the spanner and column titles and have the table number with *continued* at the top of the page (Table 1 Continued).

<u>Quotations</u>:
A direct quotation should support, explain, or illustrate the document's purpose or conclusion. It could be evidence, a well-written explanation, or a statement requiring a response. Quotations should not be just borrowed material. Do not overuse quotations; otherwise, the reader will glance over them and the document's purpose or clarity will suffer.

Do the following when reading a source and a direct quotation might be included in your document:

- Document the source information.
- Record it in a separate "quotations" area of the document where it may be evaluated with other direct quotations before inclusion into your document.
- Double-check the wording, spelling, and punctuation.

When a direct quotation is incorporated into your document, decide the following:

- Should it be run-in or block formatted?
- How will it be worked into the flow of the running text?
- How will the source be cited?

Run-In or Block Format:
The decision between a run-in or block-formatted quotation depends on quotation length. Format a short quotation as a run-in quotation (within the running text), and format a long quotation as a block quotation (separated and indented from the running text). The difference between a short and long quotation is arbitrary.

	Use Run-In Format	Use Block Format
CMOS	Publisher decides[1]	Publisher decides[1]
MLA	4 or fewer lines[2]	More than 4 lines
GRM	3 or fewer lines	More than 3 lines
APA	Fewer than 40 words	40 or more words

[1] Block format recommended when a quotation is hundreds of words, two or more paragraphs, or two or more lines of poetry.

[2] For poetry, use run-in format if three or fewer lines.

A forty-word quotation in APA format on 8½-by-11-inch paper is about three lines. Similarly, a three-line quotation in MLA format is about 40 words, and a four-line quotation is about 53 words. Block format is recommended when the direct quotation is

- Forty (40) or more words.
- Two or more complete or partial paragraphs.

Run-In Format. Place the direct quotation within the running text. Enclose the direct quotation in double quotation marks, separated it from the sentence in most situations by a comma or colon, and place a source citation after it.

- Judge DeSoto gave the jury excellent instructions: "Gather facts and decide the case in the deliberation room".[1]
  - In-text citation: ". . . room" (Clark 1998, 19).
- Many disagree with Johnson that humans are "just evolved animals"[1] and see a divine origin.
  - In-text citation: ". . . animals" (88) and . . ."

See pages 73 to 76 for quotations marks with direct quotations, quotation marks with another punctuation marks, and more examples of run-in formatted direct quotations.

Block Format. Separate and indent a block-formatted direct quotation from the running text in the following manner:

- **Separation**. Begin the quotation on a new line. Do not insert a space before or after the quotation (GRM inserts a space before and after a quotation). After a quotation, indent the running text when a new paragraph follows or start at the left margin when the paragraph continues.
- **Indentation**. Indent the entire quotation a half inch from the left margin. GRM also indents the quotation a half inch from the right margin.
- **No Quotation Marks**. Do not enclose the direct quotation in double quotation marks.
- **Paragraphing**. Paragraph breaks follow the original quotation. Separate subsequent paragraphs with a space or indent the first line.
- **Poetry Overrun**. Place any poetry-line overrun on a new line and indent the width of a capital M.

Set off a block formatted quotation from the running text with punctuation based on the introductory element. Use a colon or period with an independent clause. Use a colon when the independent clause contains the phrases "as follows" or "the following." Use a comma with a signal phrase (Rule 32) or with syntax requiring a comma. Use no punctuation when the direct quotation grammatically continues the introductory element and syntax does not require punctuation.

<u>Example 1:</u>
An independent clause introduces this block quotation.

> Indent the quotation and do not insert a space between the introduction and block quotation. Do not enclose the direct quotation in quotation marks.
>
> Paragraph breaks follow the original quotation. Separate subsequent paragraphs with a space or indent the first line.[1]

When the paragraph continues (this example), do not insert a space after the direct quotation and start at the left margin.

<u>Example 2:</u>
A comma introduces this block quotation because of syntax, and a new paragraph follows the quotation. The author stated,

> Indent the entire direct quotation a half inch from the left margin. GRM also indents the quotation a half inch from the right margin. Place any poetry-line overrun on a new line and indent the width of a capital M.[1]

Do not insert a space after the block quotation, and indent the new paragraph. When the document uses a space between paragraphs, insert a space after the quotation and start the running text at the left margin.

<u>Example 3:</u>
No punctuation introduces this block quotation. Style books agree with *The Chicago Manual of Style* that

> two independent clauses separated by a coordinating conjunction (and, but) are separated by a comma. Do not commit a common punctuation error by separating a compound predicate in a simple sentence with a comma unless a misreading is likely. (Wick 2021, 9)

Omitted Material. Use an ellipsis to show omitted material within a direct quotation (Rule 51). Add a period before an ellipsis to show the words before and after the ellipsis form a complete sentence, even if parts of the sentences are omitted.

Do not use an ellipsis before the first word of a quotation or after the last word of a quotation unless the sentence is in MLA style or is intentionally left incomplete.

- "The accident was caused by . . . the defendant."
- "The accident was caused by driver error. . . . In this case, the evidence points to the defendant."
  - Complete sentences before and after the ellipsis.
- The paragraph begins, "The contract term is . . ."
  - The sentence is intentionally incomplete.

Inserted Material. Use brackets to enclose a change, addition, or comment within a direct quotation (Rule 50). See "Allowable Changes" for examples of inserted material.

When adding emphasis to a direct quotation with italics or boldface, note the change with a parenthetical comment following the quotation ("Italics added" or similar) or in the source citation.

Allowable Changes. Direct quotations should exactly match the original wording, spelling, number style, capitalization, and punctuation—even if the original is incorrect.

Enclose all changes in brackets (Rule 50). However, the following changes are always allowable without brackets or explanation:

- Change double quotation marks to single quotation marks in a run-in quotation.
- Remove footnotes or endnote callouts. However, keep parenthetical comments or references.
- Change en dash or em dash format, including deleting spaces and changing hyphens to en dash or em dash.
- Change long *s* to modern *s* in older documents.

Examples of brackets for changes, additions, or comments:

- Judge DeSoto gave the jury excellent instructions: "[G]ather facts and decide the [attempted murder] case in the deliberation room."[1]
- "This store [in New York City] is the busiest in the state,"[1] said the company representative.
- On the witness stand, the Latin professor had only one answer to the accusations: "Errare humanum est [to err is human]."[1]
- The protestor posted on Twitter, "Gather at 9 tomorrow [January 6, 2021] at the Capit[o]l" (*Sacramento Bee*, 10 January 2021, 4A).

The following changes are allowable without brackets or explanation in APA style or for a general audience (CMOS and AP). Brackets are required for MLA style, legal documents, or documents involving textual or historical analysis.

- Change the quotation's initial letter to uppercase or lowercase to fit the sentence syntax.
- Change or omit the end punctuation mark to fit the sentence syntax.
- Correct obvious typographical errors, like misspellings.
  - Spelling, punctuation, and grammar errors in older documents are usually retained. For an isolated quotation, a correction or modernization is best stated in a footnote or parenthetical comment. For document-wide corrections or modernization, include a comment in the introduction.

Sic. Use "[*sic*]" (Latin for "in this manner") after a word to show the direct quotation accurately reproduces a spelling or grammar error in the original. Write *sic* in italics unless the document is in MLA style.

Only use *sic* if the error is likely to confuse the reader. Instead of using *sic*, consider inserting clarifying words in brackets or adding a footnote or parenthetical comment.

Syntactical Fit of Quotation:
When combining a direct quotation with the running text, the combination should be smooth, grammatically correct, and ideally free of brackets.

Two common combination problems are a mismatched verb tense (quotation versus running text) and an ambiguous pronoun in the direct quotation. To solve these problems

- revise the running text.
- move the direct quotation's starting or ending point to remove brackets or to provide a better combination.

Use brackets only when necessary. For a mismatched verb tense, bracket the changed syllable or replace with a bracketed verb (first bullet below). For an ambiguous pronoun, add a bracketed clarifying word or replace with a bracketed noun (second bullet below).

Use a bracketed replacement word for most writing situations. Use a bracketed syllable or clarifying word for MLA style, legal documents, or documents involving textual or historical analysis.

- According to Bushman, a bad historian "[fails] to separate opinions from fact."
  - or "... historian "fail[s] to ..."
- According to Bushman, "[Bad historians] fail to separate opinions from fact."
  - or " ... Bushman, "They [bad historians] fail ..."

Source Citation:
A source citation follows a direct quotation as either a footnote callout or as an in-text citation The format depends on the document's style guide (see Source Citation section).

Place a footnote after the closing quotation mark and after any punctuation except a dash.

Placed an in-text source citation for a run-in formatted quotation after the closing quotation mark and before any punctuation. For a block formatted quotation, placed an in-text source citation after the quotation's last line and after the terminal punctuation.

<u>Source Citation:</u>
A document must identify the borrowed or influential sources of opinions and information. Commonly known facts or opinions, like dates of major historical events, require no source citation. A source citation gives the reader the necessary information to identify and consult the source. It also adds credibility and acknowledges the work of others.

Express an opinion or information from another source using different words and sentence structure. This is called paraphrase. The direct borrowing words, even a keyword or short phrase, must be enclosed in quotation marks.

A source citation is required when your document

- uses a direct quotation.
- uses or adapts data from a table, chart, graph, image, figure, or diagram.
- uses paraphrase to express information from another source that is not common knowledge.
- uses paraphrase to express an idea, opinion, or theory from another person that is not common knowledge.

Record the source information in the document's Notes or Bibliography section when a source is first consulted. Every time a source is consulted, note the source in the running text. A quick parenthetical note that can be edited out is better than nothing because recording a source while writing the first draft is easier than finding it during editing.

Omitting a source citation is plagiarism. Intentional plagiarism is the deliberate presentation of another person's idea, opinion, or information as one's own work. Unintentional plagiarism is the unplanned absence of a source citation through carelessness during research or writing.

At the other end of the spectrum, source citation clutter is too many source references in a sentence or paragraph. To prevent source citation clutter, combine sources into a single reference. Order the sources as they appear in running text separated with semicolons.

Notes and Bibliography System:
CMOS is known for its notes and bibliography system. MLA and APA use an in-text source citation system (see Appendix C). A source is cited with a superscript number in the running text (example[1]) that points to a footnote at the bottom of the page or to an endnote at the end of the document.

The choice of using footnotes or endnotes is decided by the author, publisher, or instructor. When endnotes comprise more than three pages, add a page header of "Notes to" plus the applicable page numbers (Notes to Pages 4–15).

The notes and bibliography system has four components.

- **Note Number**. Use sequential, superscript numbers in the running text (example[1] and example[2]). Place the number (1) after the closing quotation marks for a direct quotation or (2) at the end of a sentence or clause. Also, place the number after any punctuation marks except a dash.

  Because numbers cannot repeat or occur out of order, repeat a citation. When references would appear in the same place (example[1,2]), combine them into a single reference (example[1]) and separated the different source citations with semicolons in the footnote or endnote.

- **Full Note** (or Full Citation). The footnote or endnote contains all necessary source information: author's name, work title, publication date, and so on.

- **Shortened Note** (or Shortened Citation). The footnote or endnote contains only the author's last name, shortened work title (four or fewer words), and applicable page numbers.

- **Bibliography**. A bibliography contains all the works cited in the footnotes or endnotes. It may also contain other consulted works.

  Alphabetize the works by author's last name. Each entry contains all necessary source information: author's name, work title, publication date, and so on. When an author has more than one listed work, alphabetize the author's works by the work title.

Use these four components in one of two ways.

- **Notes with a Bibliography**. All footnotes or endnotes are shortened notes. The reader may refer to the bibliography for further source information.

- **Notes without a Bibliography**. The first footnote or endnote to a specific work is a full note. All subsequent footnotes or endnotes to the same work are shortened notes.

Bibliography:
A bibliography contains all the works cited in the footnotes or endnotes. It may also contain other consulted works. Each entry for a work contains all necessary source information. Format a bibliography in the following manner:

- Alphabetize the works by the author's last name.
- Begin the first line of an entry at the left margin.
- Indent any runover a half inch.
- Do not use a space between entries.
- When an author has more than one listed work, alphabetize the author's works by the work title.
- Use a 3-em dash (———) in place of the author's name for all subsequent works by the same author

Example Bibliography:

Henley, Greta. *Grammar: A Reference for Teachers*. New York: Penguin, 2004.
Smith, Martin. *Essential Grammar*. Edited by Allison Jones. Chicago: Random House, 2001.
Wick, Kenneth. *The Court Reporter's Reference of Realtime Conflicts*, 2nd ed. CreateSpace, 2013.
———. *The Essential 99 Punctuation Rules for Court Reporters: Reference Edition*. Amazon, 2019
———. *The Essential 99 Punctuation Rules for Court Reporters: Workbook*. Amazon, 2019.
Zimmerman, Audrey. *The Economics of Education*. Cambridge: Cambridge University Press, 2003.

Four things are needed to create a source citation:

- Author's name
- Work title
- Publication date
- Publication details

The necessary publication details depend on the source type. Therefore, record all publication details that apply.

- **Book**: Publisher, city of publication, editor, translator, edition number, volume number, page numbers, repository location, and DOI/URL.
- **Book Chapter**: Book title, book author, publisher, city of publication, editor, translator, edition number, volume number, page numbers, repository location, and DOI/URL.
- **Journal** or **Magazine**: Journal or magazine name, volume number, issue number, publication date, page numbers, repository location, and DOI/URL.
- **Newspaper**: Newspaper name, publication date, starting page number, repository location, and DOI/URL.
- **Web Page**: Website name, URL, and access date.
- **Lecture** or **Presentation**: Event name, event location (venue name, city, and state), slide number, time marker (hour-minute-second format), and DOI/URL.
- **Audiovisual**: Director, host, production company or organization, media type or format (film, DVD), catalog number, supplemental recording or performance information, time marker (hour-minute-second format), and DOI/URL.

Online Source:

A source consulted online must include a DOI (digital object identifier) or a URL (uniform resource locator) to the source. If the source is in a commercial database (paid access), provide a link to the database or the source's information page.

Use a DOI when available because it is a unique and permanent link to the source. For a URL, try to find a stable or permalink (permanent link) to the source.

When an online source has no publication date, include the access date in the source citation. Recording the access date, even when not used, is an excellent research habit.

A line break may be inserted in a long URL before a period, comma, hyphen, question mark, ampersand (&), equal sign (=), percent symbol (%), slash (/), tilde (~), or underline (_). A line break may also be inserted after a colon or double slash (//).

Never add a hyphen to a URL to show a line break. Starting a new line with a punctuation mark or symbol helps the reader know the URL continued from the previous line.

Shorten a long URL by removing any unnecessary ending syntax used by the web browser. Always test the revised link. The first URL may be shortened to the second URL if the source citation includes the page number of 43:

    https://www.google.com/books/edition/A_Practical_English
    _Grammar/W4kVAQAAMAAJ?hl=en&gbpv=1&dq=english
    +grammar&pg=PA43&printsec=frontcover

    https://www.google.com/books/edition/A_Practical_English
    _Grammar/W4kVAQAAMAAJ

Repository Location:
For a source with limited access, place the repository information (address, call number) as a note in the citation.

Basic Note and Bibliography and Format:
A **full note** lists the author's name, work title, publication date, and publication details separated with commas. The author's last name is written last.

A **shortened note** lists the author's last name, a shortened work title (four or fewer words), and any page numbers.

A **bibliography** entry lists the author's name, work title, publication date, and publication details separated with periods. The author's last name is written first.

Work with Two Authors:

    Full: John Smith and Robert Jones

    Short: Smith and Jones

    Biblio.: Smith, John, and Robert Jones

Work with Three Authors:

    Full: John Smith, Robert Jones, and Emma Williams

    Short: Smith, Jones, and Williams

    Biblio.: Smith, John, Robert Jones, and Emma Williams

Work with Four or More Authors:

    Full: John Smith et al.

    Short: John Smith et al.

    Biblio.: List all authors.
           (Use pattern in "Work with Three Authors.")

Book (Basic Format):

    Full: Martin Smith, *Essential Grammar* (Chicago: Random House, 2001), 110.

    Short: Smith, *Essential Grammar*, 110.

    Biblio.: Smith, Martin. *Essential Grammar*. Chicago: Random House, 2001.

Book with Editor or Translator:
Use "ed." or "trans." in a full note. Use "Edited by" or "Translated by" in the bibliography.

    Full: Martin Smith, *Essential Grammar*, ed. Allison Jones (Chicago: Random House, 2001), 110.

    Short: Smith, *Essential Grammar*, 110.

    Biblio.: Smith, Martin. *Essential Grammar*. Edited by Allison Jones. Chicago: Random House, 2001.

Book Consulted Online:
Provide a DOI (preferred) or URL to the source. If the source is in a commercial database (paid access), provide a link to the database or the source's information page.

Full: Martin Smith, *Essential Grammar*, ed. Allison Jones (Chicago: Random House, 2001), 110, https://doi.org/10.1234/8080.

Short: Smith, *Essential Grammar*, 110.

Biblio.: Smith, Martin. *Essential Grammar*. Edited by Allison Jones. Chicago: Random House, 2001. https://doi.org/10.1234/8080.

Book with Edition:

Full: Martin Smith, *Essential Grammar*, 3rd ed. (Chicago: Random House, 2009), 112.

Short: Smith, *Essential Grammar*, 112.

Biblio.: Smith, Martin. *Essential Grammar*. 3rd ed. Chicago: Random House, 2005.

Modern Edition of Book:
When the original publication details are important, include them as a note at the end of the citation.

Full: Allison Jones, *Grammar for Adults*, (Chicago: Random House, 1986), 64. First Published by University of Chicago Press in 1972.

Short: Jones, *Grammar for Adults*, 64.

Biblio.: Jones, Allison. *Grammar for Adults*. Chicago: Random House, 1986. First Published by University of Chicago Press in 1972.

Multivolume Work:
In a footnote or endnote, separate the volume number and page number with a colon.

Full: Martin Smith, *Comprehensive Grammar* (Chicago: Random House, 2009), 3:84.

Short: Smith, *Comprehensive Grammar*, 3:84.

Biblio.: Smith, Martin. *Comprehensive Grammar*. 4 vols. Chicago: Random House, 2009.

Chapter in a Book:
Use "in" before the book title. Include the chapter's page range in the bibliography.

Full: Leah Smith, "Common Comma Errors," in *English Punctuation*, 2nd ed., ed. Robin Jones (New York: Penguin Press, 2015), 114.

Short: Smith, "Common Comma Errors," 114.

Biblio.: Smith, Leah. "Common Comma Errors." In *English Punctuation*, 2nd ed., edited by Robin Jones, 112–128. New York: Penguin Press, 2015.

Journal Article (Basic Format):
Follow the journal name with the volume and issue number. Enclose the date in parentheses, and a colon precedes the page range. When an issue has no date, enclose the issue number in parentheses: *Grammar Quarterly* 5 (2): 7. Include the article's page range in the bibliography.

Full: John Smith, "The Exclamation Mark," *Grammar Quarterly* 5, no. 2 (March 2005):7.

Short: Smith, "Exclamation Mark," 7.

Biblio.: Smith, John. "The Exclamation Mark." *Grammar Quarterly* 5, no. 2 (March 2005): 5–8.

Journal Article Consulted Online.
Provide a DOI (preferred) or URL to the source. If the source is in a commercial database (paid access), provide a link to the database or an information page.

Full: Linda Jones, "The Exclamation Mark Revisited," *Grammar Quarterly* 19, no.3 (Fall 2019): 11–14, https://www.grquarterly.com/journal/19-3/exclamation-mark-revisited.

Short: Jones, "Exclamation Mark Revisited," 12.

Biblio.: Jones, Linda. "The Exclamation Mark Revisited." *Grammar Quarterly* 19, no.3 (Fall 2019): 11–14. https://www.grquarterly.com/journal /19-3/exclamation-mark-revisited.

Newspaper or Magazine Article:
Format a magazine article with volume and issue information like a journal article. For an article accessed online, provide the web link (see "Journal Article Consulted Online"). Because page numbers for a newspaper article are likely not consecutive, reference only the first or relevant page number.

Full: Angelina Rodriguez, "Practical Sentences," *The New York Times*, October 28, 2017, C5.

Short: Rodriguez, "Practical Sentences," C5.

Biblio.: Rodriguez, Angelina. "Practical Sentences." *The New York Times*, October 28, 2017.

Web Page:
For a web page updated since the original publication date, use "updated" or "last modified" with the modification date as the publication date. When a web page has no publication date, use "accessed" with the access date.

If a web page is no longer available or important information was changed or deleted, include the changed text or a comment at the end of the citation (Web page no longer available; Text changed from "115 injured" to "3 dead and 123 injured.")

Full: Wendy Jones, "Writing Reports," *Grammar Quarterly,* published July 21, 2020, https://www.grquarterly.com/resources/wr-reports.

         Victor Nunes, "Outlining," *Grammar Quarterly,* accessed February 16, 2020, https://www.grquarterly.com/resources /outlining.

Short: Jones, "Writing Reports."
         Nunes, "Outlining."

Biblio.: Jones, Wendy. "Writing Reports." *Grammar Quarterly*. Published July 21, 2020. https://www.grquarterly.com/resources/wr-reports.

         Nunes. Victor. "Outlining." *Grammar Quarterly*. Accessed February 16, 2020. https://www.grquarterly.com/resources/outlinine.

Lecture or Presentation

Include relevant supplemental information, like slide number and DOI/URL.

Full: William Jones, "The Direction of Capitalization," The 4th Annual Grammar Convention, New York, December 10, 2017.

Short: Jones, "Direction of Capitalization."

Biblio.: Jones, William. "The Direction of Capitalization." The 4th Annual Grammar Convention, New York, December 10, 2017.

Audiovisual:

Include relevant supplemental information: media type or format, catalog number, production or performance information, time marker to a specific location (hour-minute-second format), and DOI/URL.

Film:

Full: Milos Forman, dir., *One Flew Over the Cuckoo's Nest* (Los Angeles: United Artists, 1975), film.

Short: Forman, *One Flew Over.*

Biblio.: Forman, Milos, dir. *One Flew Over the Cuckoo's Nest.* Los Angeles: United Artists, 1975. Film.

Web Video:

Full: Mary Clark, host, "Practical Grammar," August 23, 2003, University of English, Video, https://youtube.com/923u03h.

Short: Clark, "Practical Grammar."

Biblio.: Clark, Mary, host. "Practical Grammar." University of English, August 23, 2003. Video. https://youtube.com/923u03h.

Music Album:

    Full: David Bowie, *Blackstar,* Columbia Records, 2016, compact disc.

    Short: Bowie, *Blackstar.*

    Biblio.: Bowie, David. *Blackstar.* Columbia Records, 2016. Compact disc.

Song:

    Full: Beyoncé, "Pretty Hurts," *Beyoncé*, Columbia Records, 2016, compact disc, https://www.beyonce.com/album/beyonce/songs.

    Short: Beyoncé, "Pretty Hurts."

    Biblio.: Beyoncé. "Pretty Hurts." *Beyoncé.* Columbia Records, 2016. Compact disc, https://www.beyonce.com/album/beyonce/songs.

Example of Footnotes and Endnotes:
The following two paragraphs and the bottom of this page show footnotes in full note format. The next page shows the same notes as endnotes and as a bibliography with applicable shortened notes.

List footnotes at the bottom of the page beneath a short horizontal line.[1] Indent the first line a half inch, and align any runover with the left margin. Note numbers are regular size, not superscript.[2]

Place all endnotes at the end of the document and before the bibliography.[3] List the endnotes after a centered "Notes" heading, and format the endnotes like footnotes.[4]

---

1. Martin Smith, *Essential Grammar* (Chicago: Random House, 2001), 110.

2. Allison Jones, *Grammar for Adults*, (Chicago: Random House, 1986), 64. First Published by University of Chicago Press in 1972.

3. Smith, *Essential Grammar*, 78.

4. Linda Jones, "The Exclamation Mark Revisited," *Grammar Quarterly* 19, no.3 (Fall 2019): 11–14, https://www.grquarterly.com/journal/19-3/exclamation-mark-revisited.

Notes

1. Martin Smith, *Essential Grammar* (Chicago: Random House, 2001), 110.

2. Allison Jones, *Grammar for Adults*, (Chicago: Random House, 1986), 64. First Published by University of Chicago Press in 1972.

3. Smith, *Essential Grammar*, 78.

4. Linda Jones, "The Exclamation Mark Revisited," *Grammar Quarterly* 19, no.3 (Fall 2019): 11–14, https://www.grquarterly.com/journal/19-3/exclamation-mark-revisited.

Bibliography

Jones, Allison. *Grammar for Adults*. Chicago: Random House, 1986. First Published by University of Chicago Press in 1972.

Jones, Linda. "The Exclamation Mark Revisited." *Grammar Quarterly* 19, no.3 (Fall 2019): 11–14. https://www.grquarterly.com/journal/19-3/exclamation-mark-revisited.

Smith, Martin. *Essential Grammar*. Edited by Allison Jones. Chicago: Random House, 2001.

When the document includes a bibliography, use shortened notes for footnotes or endnotes. The shortened notes for the previous footnotes or endnotes examples are:

1. Smith, *Essential Grammar*, 78.
2. Jones, *Grammar for Adults*, 64.
3. Smith, *Essential Grammar*, 78.
4. Jones, "Exclamation Mark Revisited," 13.

a, an:
Use "a" before a word or abbreviation beginning with a consonant or long u sound (a dog; a girl; a unit; a U.S. law). Use "an" before a word beginning with a vowel sound, except long u (an assignment, an effect, an hour, an IBM product).

affect, effect:
Affect is a verb often meaning "to influence or change." The verb also means "to pretend in feeling or manner." In psychology, *affect* is a noun meaning "feeling or emotion."

Effect is as a noun often meaning "result or outcome." When used as a verb, *effect* means "to cause or bring about."

among, between:
Use *between* when referring to two people or things (between Maria and Josh; between managers and employees). Use *among* when referring to more than two people or things (among five clients; among the students).

amount, number:
Use *amount* with mass nouns, and use *number* with count nouns. A mass noun is something that cannot be counted and usually has no plural form (garbage, money, traffic). A count noun is something that can be counted and usually has a plural form (car, computer, key).

attain, obtain:
These words are synonyms in informal writing. In formal writing, *attain* means "to reach or accomplish a goal, usually by effort" (attain a medical degree). *Obtain* means "to gain possession of something" (obtain information; obtain a letter).

can, could:
Can means "to be able to" and conveys certainty (we can fix it). *Could* conveys uncertainty in the present tense or a conditional statement in the past tense (with at least an hour, we could solve the problem).

can, may:
Can shows physical or mental ability (she can swim). *May* shows permission or possibility (may I swimming? No, you may not). In informal writing, *can* may also express permission (can I go swimming? Yes, you can).

continual, continuous:
Continuous means "uninterrupted," and *continual* means "steady repetition." Often the adverb *continuously* is used when *continually* should be used.

farther, further:
These words are synonyms in informal writing. *Farther* refers to a greater physical distance (we walked farther than anticipated). *Further* refers to a greater degree or extent (this requires further discussion).

if, whether:
The word *if* introduces a conditional statement (if you find the wallet, call me). *Whether* introduces alternatives (let me know whether you are going to the movies or staying home). The phrase *whether or not* introduces the alternatives yes and no (let me know whether or not you are going to the movies).

in, into:
Use *in* to show location or limits (in California, in the car). Use *into* to show inclusion or the motion of entry (entered into an agreement; ran into the apartment).

lay, lie:
Lay (past: laid; present participle: laying) means "to put or place." The verb always has a direct object (lay the <u>keys</u> on the kitchen table).

Lie (past: lay; present participle: lain) means "to rest or recline." The verb does not have a direct object (the keys lie on the table).

less, fewer:
Use *less* with mass nouns (less garbage), and use *fewer* with count nouns (fewer keys). See *amount, number.*

may, might:
May shows what is possible or likely factual (she may win the race because of her lead). *Might* shows uncertainty or contrary to fact (I might have taken a wrong turn). The past tense of *may* is *might*.

neither, nor:
Both *neither* and *nor* negate alternatives (neither steak nor crab is on the menu; neither snow nor rain nor heat will prevent a mail carrier). Typically, there are only two alternatives (neither cars nor trucks). The alternatives should be parallel (see page 28), and the verb agrees with the alternative next to the last *nor* (see "or" on page 44).

on, onto:
Onto implies movement. Use *onto* when the words *up* or *down* could be sensibly (but only mentally) added before *on*.

ought, should:
Ought shows a stronger sense of duty than *should,* and it is used with an infinitive (you ought to go to the wedding).

should, would:
Should expresses obligation (I should go to work) or a condition in an *if* clause (if I should win the lottery, I will quit my job). *Would* expresses a customary action (as a teenager, I would read for hours) or willingness in an *if* clause (if I would study more, I could get better grades).

who, whom:
Use *who* for the subject of the sentence (she is the one who will win the election; who drove the car?). Use *whom* for the object of the sentence or with the object of a preposition (I could not figure out from whom the article quoted; whom should we test?).

To decide between using *who* or *whom*, replace the word with a pronoun (*he, she, him*, or *her)*. If *he* or *she* sounds better, use *who*. If *him* or *her* sounds better, use *whom*.

Appendix A: Grammar Reference

1. Parts of English Speech
English has eight parts of speech.

1. Noun	A person (Jim), place (ocean), or thing (table)
2. Pronoun	Substitute for a noun (he, she, it)
3. Verb	Expresses action (to run) or state of being (is)
4. Adjective	Modifies a noun (big, red)
5. Adverb	Modifies a verb, adjective, or another adverb (slowly, not)
6. Conjunction	Joins words, phrases, or clauses (and, but)
7. Preposition	Connects a noun or pronoun to another word (on, above, over)
8. Interjection	Expresses feeling (wow, damn)

1-1. Word Order
The expected word order in an English sentence is subject, then verb, and then object.

Verb:	What is the action?
Subject:	Who or what is doing the action?
Direct Object:	The *who* or *what* about the verb.
Indirect Object:	The *to whom* or *for whom* about the verb.

- She kicked the ball.

Verb (action):	kicked
Subject (who kicked?):	she
Direct Object (kicked what?):	the ball

- I gave him money.

Verb (action):	gave
Subject (who gave?):	I
Direct Object (gave what?):	money
Indirect Object (gave to?):	him

2. Clauses and Phrases

A clause is a group of related words containing a subject and predicate (verb plus any modifiers and complements). Clauses are classified as either independent or dependent.

A phrase is a group of related words without a subject, a predicate, or both. Common phrase types include prepositional phrases and verbal phrases.

An elliptical clause is a grammatically incomplete clause that represents a complete clause. It lacks a subject, a predicate, or both. Any missing element is understood from the context.

3. Independent Clause

An independent clause is a clause (subject and predicate) that does <u>not</u> begin with a subordinating conjunction (Section 5). It could stand alone as a simple sentence.

- She kicked the ball.
- I gave him money for a loan.

4. Dependent Clause

A dependent clause is a clause (subject and predicate) that begins with a subordinating conjunction (Section 5). A dependent clause modifies an independent clause and functions as a noun, adjective, or adverb. It cannot stand alone as a simple sentence.

- Edward tripped **because he did not tie his shoe**.
- **When I received my paycheck**, I paid the rent.

A relative clause is a dependent clause that begins with a relative pronoun (that, who, which, whom, whose). A relative clause functions as an adjective.

- I live with a nice guy **who is my chemistry lab partner**.
- Tim spent the $1,000 **that was for the rent**.

5. Subordinating Conjunctions

A subordinating conjunction begins and joins a dependent clause to an independent clause.

Common Subordinating Conjunctions:

after	inasmuch	till
although	in case	**though**
as	in case that	unless
as far as	in order	**until**
as if	in order that	**when**
as long as	lest	whenever
as soon as	now that	**where**
as though	once	whereas
because	only if	wherever
before	provided	**whether**
even if	provided that	**which**
even though	rather than	**while**
how	**since**	**who**
if	**so**	whoever
if only	so that	whom
if when	**than**	whomever
if then	**that**	whose

- I made dinner **after** I went to the store.
- **Whenever** I see bad punctuation, I scream inside.

Subordination:

A subordinating conjunction joins and subordinates a clause to an independent clause. The subordinated clause shows its ideas or details are less important than those in the independent clause. Subordination often shows cause, condition, purpose, size, location, details of time, and so on.

By contrast, a coordinating conjunction (and, but, or) joins related independent clauses. The ideas or details in the coordinated clauses have equal importance.

6. Coordinating Conjunctions

Seven coordinating conjunctions join words, phrases, or clauses of equal status: word to word, phrase to phrase, or clause to clause. They spell the acronym FANBOYS.

for	but
and	or
nor	yet
	so

- For three days, I ate only <u>bread</u> **and** <u>water</u>.   (words)
- The question is, <u>To be</u> **or** <u>not to be</u>.   (phrases)
- <u>I went shopping</u>, **but** <u>the stores were closed</u>.   (clauses)

7. Conjunctive Adverbs and Transitional Expressions

Conjunctive adverbs and transitional expressions join and show the relationship between independent clauses.

Common Conjunctive Adverbs and Transitional Expressions:

accordingly	in other words	plus
afterward	in summary	presently
also	indeed	presumably
although	instead	primarily
as a result	last	rather
at that time	likewise	regardless
besides	meanwhile	**second**
certainly	more important	similarly
consequently	moreover	**so**
finally	needless to say	still
first	nevertheless	that is
for example	**next**	**then**
further	nonetheless	thereafter
furthermore	notwithstanding	**therefore**
generally	**now**	**thus**
hence	obviously	to illustrate
however	on the contrary	ultimately
in addition	on the other hand	usually
in comparison	originally	yet
in conclusion	otherwise	
in contrast	perhaps	

- Tony joined the meeting late. **Nevertheless**, he beat the boss by thirty seconds.
- I arrived early for the test; **however**, I forgot a pencil.

7-1. Parenthetical Expressions

A parenthetical expression is a comment or explanation expressing an opinion or attitude. It could be removed from the sentence without affecting the meaning.

Common Parenthetical Expressions:

apparently	obviously	to be honest
as I see it	**of course**	to tell the truth
in fact	**oh**	**unfortunately**
in my opinion	personally	**well**
no	sitting here today	**yes**

- **Unfortunately**, I do not recall.
- Mary has a great memory. **In fact**, she still remembers her first cell phone number.

8. Prepositional Phrase

A preposition connects a noun or pronoun to another word or sentence element. A prepositional phrase begins with a preposition, and it functions as an adjective or adverb.

Common Prepositions:

about	behind	**in**	outside
above	below	in addition to	**over**
across	beneath	inside	**through**
after	beside	instead of	throughout
against	between	**into**	**to**
along	beyond	near	toward
among	**by**	next to	under
around	**down**	**of**	underneath
as	during	**off**	**up**
at	except	**on**	upon
because	except for	onto	**with**
before	for	on top of	within
	from	**out**	without

- The book **on the table** is worth $100.
- He ran **around the corner**.

9. Verbal Phrase

A verbal phrase begins with a *–ing*, *–ed*, or *to* plus an infinitive verb (shopping, shopped, to shop). It functions as an adjective, adverb, or noun.

- **Shopping for clothes** is relaxing after a long day.
- **Determined to past the typing test**, the student planned many hours of practice.
- Anthony designs all city parks **to ensure the efficient use of space**.

To test for a verbal phrase, change the sentence tense from present to past or from past to present. If the verb tense does <u>not</u> need to be changed, the phrase is a verbal phrase.

<u>Example Test for a Verbal Phrase</u>:
Shopping for clothes is relaxing after a long day.

- Test: Change the sentence to past tense.
  - *Shopping for clothes* was relaxing after a long day.
- Result: No change to *shopping for clothes*. Therefore, it is a verbal phrase.

10. Essential Element

An essential (or restrictive) element is a word, phrase, or clause needed for the meaning of the sentence. It defines or restricts the meaning of the element it modifies. **Essential elements are never separated with punctuation**.

- My cousin **who arrived from Idaho** is visiting me through the weekend.
  - The clause defines which cousin.

- I got a flu **before I was involved in the car accident**.
  - The clause limits *I got a flu*. It defines which flu.

11. Nonessential Element

A nonessential (or nonrestrictive) element is a word, phrase, or clause <u>not</u> needed for the meaning of the sentence. It only adds information and could be removed without affecting the meaning of the sentence. The element the nonessential element modifies is already defined or restricted.

Sometimes the distinction between an essential and nonessential element is insignificant or is difficult to determine. **Nonessential elements are always separated with punctuation**.

- Mary, **who is my cousin from Idaho**, is visiting me through the weekend.
  - The relative clause only adds information because Mary is probably known from the context.

- I lost my job last Tuesday, **before I was involved in a car accident**.
  - The dependent clause only adds information. It does not define *last Tuesday*.

<u>Nonessential Element Test:</u>
To test for a nonessential element, remove it from the sentence. Did the meaning of the sentence change? If it did not, the element is nonessential. If it did, the element is essential.

- Kathy, **in my English class**, is from China.
  - The phrase only adds information because the meaning of the sentence did not change when it was removed (Kathy is from China). This assumes Kathy is known from the context. Therefore, the element is nonessential, and it is separated with punctuation.

- The students **in my English class** are from China.
  - The phrase is essential because without it the meaning of the sentence changes. The sentence without the phrase is about all students, not just the English class students. Therefore, the element is essential, and it is not separated with punctuation.

Appendix B: Unnecessary Words and Phrases

List 1: Long Phrases

Original	Revised
a good/great deal of	many, much
a large (Word) of	many, much
a large part/percentage of	many, much
a large portion of	many
a large/small number of	many/some
a lot of	many
a number of	many, several, some
a significant portion of	many, most
a small (Word) of	some
a small part/percentage of	some
a smaller amount of	fewer
a wide range of	many
an absence of	lacking
an additional amount of	more
an amount of	some
an overwhelming majority	most
arising/coming from the fact that	because
as a result of	because of, from
as far as it/this is concerned	for
as well as	also, and
associated with	if
at all times	always
at the end of	after
at the present time	now
at the same time	while, (Remove)
at this point in time	now
by itself	alone
by means of	by
down to	down
due to the fact that	because
during the time that	while
fact that	because
for the reason that	because
form the point of view	for

Original	Revised
from the standpoint of	for
half of all the (Word)	half the (Word)
in a few minutes	soon
in a timely fashion	soon
in accordance with your request	as you requested
in addition to	with
in advance of	before
in association with	with
in back of	behind
in cases that	if, when
in certain situations	occasionally
in close proximity	near, close, about
in combination with	with
in connection with	about, related to
in consideration of the fact that	because
in instances in which	if, when
in isolation	alone
in opposition too	against
in order to	to
in recent history	lately, recently
in regards to	about, on
in relation to	about, on
in respect to	about, on
in spite of the fact that	although
in such a way that	so that
in support of	for, to
in the case of	concerning
in the course of	during
in the direction of	toward
in the event that	if
in the final analysis	finally
in the general vicinity	here
in the near future	soon
in the neighborhood of	about, close, near
in the not so distant future	soon
in the role of	as
in the vicinity	near
in thickness	thick
in this day and age	today

Original	Revised
in today's society/world	now
in view of the fact that	because
involved in	of
many of the	many
not the same	different
on a regular basis	regularly
on an annual basis	annually
on the basis of	because of, by, on
on the other hand	but
quite a few	many
the majority of	many, most
the vast majority of	most
to a large extent	largely
to the extent that	as much as
to the fullest extent possible	fully
toward the direction of	toward
until such time as	until
up to	up
virtually all	most
when the (Word) was over	after the (Word)
with reference to the fact that	about, concerning
with regards to	about, concerning
with respect to	about, for, from, on

List 2: Parenthetical Expressions and Empty Words

Original	Revised
(Word) of the (Word) Ex: many of the people	(Word) (Word) many people
a total of	(Remove)
actually	(Remove)
all	(Possible Removal)
all things considered	(Remove)
as a matter of fact	(Remove)
as far as I'm concerned	(Remove)
as to	(Remove)
at that time	(Remove)
basically	(Remove)

Original	Revised
because of the fact that	because
both	(Possible Removal)
by their nature	(Remove)
certainly	(Remove)
clearly	(Remove)
despite the fact that	although, despite
down	(Possible Removal)
extremely	(Remove)
for all intents and purposes	(Remove)
for the most part	(Remove)
for your information	(Remove)
fortunately	(Remove)
fundamentally	(Remove)
generally	(Remove)
hopefully	(Remove)
in a manner of speaking	(Remove)
in a nutshell	briefly, (Remove)
in appears that	(Remove)
in fact	(Remove)
in general	(Remove)
in my opinion	(Remove)
in that regard	(Remove)
it goes without saying	(Remove)
it is apparent that	(Remove)
it is worth noting	(Remove)
it seems that	(Remove)
it should be pointed out that	(Remove)
it would appear that	(Remove)
just	(Possible Removal)
know as	(Remove)
last but not least	(Remove)
more or less	(Remove)
mostly	(Remove)
naturally	(Remove)
needless to say	(Remove)
of course	(Remove)
on the part	(Remove)
on the whole	(Remove)
out	(Possible Removal)

Original	Revised
pretty (intensifier)	(Remove)
quite	(Remove)
rather	(Remove)
really	(Remove)
severely	(Remove)
so-called	(Remove)
some	(Possible Removal)
some of the	some
suddenly	(Remove)
that	(Possible Removal)
the (Empty Word) of Ex: the concept of	(Possible Removal)
the (Empty Word) of (Word) Ex: the concept of sound	(Word) sound
The (Verb) of (Word) Ex: the making of cloths	(–ing Verb) (Word) making cloth
the amount of	(Remove)
the area of	(Remove)
the case of	(Remove)
the character of	(Remove)
the concept of	(Remove)
the existence of	(Remove)
the fact remains that	(Remove)
the fact that	(Remove)
the level of	(Remove)
the method of	(Remove)
the number of	(Remove)
the practice of	(Remove)
the principal of	(Remove)
the process of	(Remove)
the purpose of	(Remove)
the question of	(Remove)
the role of	(Remove)
the scope of	(Remove)
the state of	(Remove)
up	(Possible Removal)
very	(Remove)
what this means is	(Remove)

List 3: Long Verb Phrases

Original	Revised
appears to be	is
are (–ing Verb) Ex: are making	(Verb) make
are in possession of	have
arrive at a compromise	compromise
arrive at a conclusion	conclude
arrive at a decision	decide
by way of (–ing Verb) Ex: by way of showing	to (Verb) to show
has a difference of opinion	disagrees
has come to my attention that	I learned
has in his/her possession	has, possesses
has the ability to	can
has the access to	can access
has to do with	concerns, regards
have an impact on	affect
have got to	must
in an effort to	to
is (Word) of/to Ex: is equal to	(Word [Verb]) equals
is afraid of	fears
is because	is that
is beneficial to	benefits
is comparable to	compares to
is complimentary to	compliments
is critical of	criticizes
is descriptive of	describes
is equal to	equals
is favorable of	favors
is harmful to	harms
is in contrast to	contrasts
is in control of	controls
is in fear of	fears
is in support of	supports
is of a (Word) character/nature Ex: is of an excellent character	is (Word) is excellent

Original	Revised
is reflective of	reflects
is resistant to	resists
is suggestive of	suggests
is symbolic of	symbolizes
is typical of	typifies
it is (Word) that/which is Ex: it is rice that is	(Word) is rice is
it is recommended that	we recommend
it would be advisable to	should
made a statement saying	stated, said
make (Word [Noun]) Ex: make an attempt	(Word [Verb]) attempt
make a decision about	decide
make a distinction	distinguish
make a statement	state
make allowances	allow
make an appearance	appear
make an attempt	attempt, try
make decisions about	decide on
make mention of	mention
make progress toward	progress toward
make up my mind	decide
make/put in an appearance	appear
may have the effect of (-ing Verb) Ex: may have the effect of showing	may (Verb) may show
place a value on	value
plays a major role	contribute to, is important
predicated upon the fact that	based on
pursuant to your request	as you requested
put an end to	stop
put forward	advance
put my finger on	identify
take a look	look
take a stand for	endorse
take action	act
take advantage of	exploit
take exception to	challenge
take hold of	grasp
take into account	consider

Original	Revised
take into consideration	consider
take into custody	arrest
take offense at	resent
take place	occur
take satisfaction in	enjoy
take the position	contend
the purpose of (–ing Verb) Ex: the purpose of running	to (Verb) to run
was instrumental in (–ing Verb) Ex: was instrumental in showing	helped
was of the opinion that	believed, thought, said
was witness to	witnessed, saw
will be able to	can
will be instrumental in (–ing Verb) Ex: will be instrumental in showing	will help
would be able to	could
would have been able to	could have

List 4: Zombie Nouns

Original	Revised
has a preference for	prefers
has an appreciation for	appreciates
has an effect on	effects
has intentions of	intends
have a tendency to	tend to
in inclusion of	including
is (Word) of/to Ex: is an example of	(Word [Verb]) exemplifies
is a contribution to	contributes to
is a demonstration of	demonstrates
is a description of	describes
is a representation of	represents
is a variant of	varies from
is an illustration of	illustrates
is an indications of	indicates

Original	Revised
is characteristic of	characterizes
is equivalent to	equals
is in conformance to	conforms to
is in need of	needs
is in opposition to	opposes
is in possession of	possesses
is indicative of	indicates
is proof of	proves
is the recipient of	receives
provide a summary of	summarize
put into effect	effect
reach a conclusion	conclude
the acceptance of	accepting
the development of	developing
the installation of	installing
the maintenance of	maintaining
the testing of	testing

List 5: Unnecessary Repetition

Original	Revised
(Number) in number Ex: Twenty in number	(Number) Twenty
alternative choice	choice
analyze in depth	analyze
basic essentials	essentials
blue/green/red in color	blue/green/red
brand new	new
circle around	circle
circular/square/rectangular in shape	circular/square/rectangular
close proximity	close
consensus of opinion	consensus
cooperate together	cooperate

Original	Revised
different and distinct	different, distinct
duplicate copy	copy
each and every	each, every
end product/result	product/result
end result	result
established standard	standard
fair and equitable	fair, equitable
few in number	few
final completion	completion
final coup de grace	coup de grace
final outcome	outcome
first and foremost	first
first began/started	began/started
first introduced	introduced
follow after	follow
free gift	gift
full and complete	full, complete
future plans	plans
have in possession	have
honest truth	truth
hope and expect	hope, expect
if and only if	if, only if
illustrative example	example
important essentials	essentials
in the past was	was
joint cooperation/agreement	cooperation/agreement
large/small in size	large/small
little child	child
make changes	change
mass exodus	exodus
must inevitably/necessarily	must
necessary essential/requirement	essential/requirement
new and improved	new, improved
new innovation	innovation

Original	Revised
one and only	only
one and the same	same
original creator/founder	creator/founder
past achievement/experience	achievement/experience
past history	history
pick and choose	pick, choose
plain and simple	plain, simple
plan ahead/in advance	plan
postpone until later	postpone
proven fact	fact
reason why	reason
regular routine	routine
repeat/return again	repeat/return
report back	report
resume again	resume
rules and regulations	rules, regulations
serious danger	danger
short summary	summary
splice together	splice
sum total	total
surround on all sides	surround
temporary stopgap	stopgap
together as a group/team	together
total annihilation	annihilation
train professional	trained, profession
violent explosion	explosion
warn in advance	warn
wholly and completely	wholly, completely
will in the future	will
will take steps to	will

Appendix C: In-Text Source Citation

CMOS, APA, and MLA each have an in-text source citation system consisting of a brief parenthetical note in the running text. The in-text citation points the reader to the bibliography section at the end of the document, called "Works Cited" in CMOS and MLA and "Reference List" in APA.

CMOS and APA provide the author's last name and publication year (author-date system). MLA provides the author's last name and page number (author-page system).

	Basic Format	Example
CMOS	(Author Year)	(Smith 2018)
APA	(Author, Year)	(Smith, 2018)
MLA	(Author Page)	(Smith 110)

The best place to insert an in-text citation is at the end of a sentence and before the period. It may also be placed at the end of a phrase or clause and before any punctuation mark. For a direct quotation, place the in-text citation after the closing quotation mark and before the period (see page 131).

When all the information in a paragraph is from the same source, one source citation at the end of the paragraph is sufficient. Order the page numbers for any direct quotations as they appear in the paragraph.

In-text citations are often written in either a narrative or parenthetical format. A narrative-formatted citation contains the author's last name in the running text and places the publication year or page number in parentheses. A parenthetical-formatted citation places both the author's last name and the publication year or page number in parentheses.

Narrative Format (MLA Format):
- Clark showed in avoiding the number thirteen that many educated adults cling to forms of folk magic (19).
- Many disagree with Johnson that humans are "just evolved animals" (88) and see a divine origin.

Parenthetical Format (APA Format):
- Educated adults often cling to various forms of folk magic, like avoiding the number thirteen (Clark, 1998).
- Many disagree that we are "just evolved animals" and see a divine origin (Johnson, 2019).

Beyond the basic format, various citation situations arise. Therefore, use the basic format and the following guidelines.

Work with Two Authors:

CMOS:	(Jones and Smith 2017)
APA:	(Jones and Smith, 2017)
MLA:	(Jones and Smith 110)

Work with Three or More Authors:

CMOS:	3: (Jones, Mann, and Smith 2015)
	4+: (Davis et al. 2019)
APA:	(Jones et al., 2015)
MLA:	(Jones et al. 110)

Work with Corporate Author:
Use the name of the corporation, organization, or association as the author's name. MLA allows shortened names.

CMOS:	(United States, Department of Labor 2019)
APA:	(United States, Department of Labor, 2019)
MLA:	(US, Dept. of Labor 110)

For a long corporate name, consider using it in the running text and defining an abbreviation. Then use the abbreviation in the citation. After defining "United States, Department of Labor" as "U.S. DOL" in the running text, the above citations would be:

CMOS:	(U.S. DOL 2019)
APA:	(U.S. DOL, 2019)
MLA:	(U.S. DOL 110)

Different Works Having Author with Same Last Name:
Use the initial of the author's first name plus the last name.

CMOS:	(R. Smith 2017)
APA:	(R. Smith, 2017)
MLA:	(R. Smith 110)

Work with Unknown Author:
Substitute the work title for the author's name. If the title is long, use an abbreviation—three or fewer words is best. The abbreviation's first word must be the same word used for alphabetization in the Works Cited or Reference List. Italicize a book title or website name, and enclose the title of a journal or website article in quotation marks.

CMOS:	("High Tide" 2018)	[Article]
APA:	(*Strengthening Youth*, 2018)	[Book]
MLA:	("Top Ten Sonnets" 4)	[Article]

Same Author with Multiple Works:
If the same author published two or more works in a single year for CMOS or APA, use a lowercase letter after the year to distinguish the works (2019a, 2019b).

MLA includes an abbreviated title after the author's name—three or fewer words is best. The abbreviation's first word must be the same word used for alphabetization in the Works Cited. Italicize a book title or website name, and enclose the title of a journal or website article in quotation marks.

CMOS:	(Smith 2017a)
APA:	(Smith, 2017a)
MLA:	(Smith, "Dancing" 30)

Work with No Publication Year:
Use "n.d." if the publication date is unknown. CMOS adds a comma for clarity.

CMOS:	(Smith, n.d.)
APA:	(Smith, n.d.)
MLA:	(Smith 110) [Basic Format]

Citation with Page Number Reference:

CMOS:	(Smith 2017, 110)
	(Smith 2017, 110–112)
APA:	(Smith 2017, p. 110)
	(Smith 2012, pp. 110–112)
MLA:	(Smith 110)
	(Smith 110–112)

Citation with Reference to a Portion of the Work:
Precede a reference to a portion of the work other than a page number with a descriptive word or abbreviation. Do not reference an e-reader page or location number. Instead, use the heading name and/or paragraph number. Use the following abbreviations:

	CMOS	APA	MLA
Volume	vol.	Volume	vol.
Section	sec.	Section	sec.
Chapter	chap.	Chapter	ch.
Paragraph	para.	para.	par.

CMOS: (Smith 2017, para. 4)
       (Smith 2017, vol. 2)
       (Smith 2017, 2:110) [volume 2, page 110]
       (Smith 2017, under "Introduction")

APA: Smith, 2017, para. 4)
       (Smith, 2017, Volume 2)
       (Smith, 2017, Table 14)
       (Smith, 2017, Musical section, para. 4)

MLA: (Smith, par. 4)
       (Smith, vol. 2)
       (Smith, vol. 2, ch. 8)
       (Smith, sec. "Introduction")

Citation with Multiple Source References:
Separate multiple references with a semicolon. CMOS and MLA references may be listed alphabetically, chronologically, or by order of importance. List APA references alphabetically. See page 169 for end-of-paragraph references.

CMOS: (Smith 2017; Jones 2019)
APA: (Jones, 2019; Smith, 2017)
MLA: (Jones 90; Smith 110)

Citation with a Note:
Separate the citation and any brief note with a semicolon.

CMOS: (Smith 2017; emphasis added)
APA: No Standard
MLA: (Smith 115; emphasis added)

Citation with Audio or Video Source:
APA and MLA include an hour-minute-second source location.
CMOS places the audio or video source location in the Works
Cited section.

    CMOS: (Jones 2019)
    APA: (Jones, 2019, 1:37:12)
    MLA: (Jones 00:37:12)

Citation to Modern Edition of a Work:
    CMOS: (Milton [1667] 1995)
    APA: (Milton, 1667/1995)
    MLA: (Milton 110 [1995])

Citation is an Indirect Reference:
An author should note when the original source cannot be
consulted. MLA abbreviates *quoted in* with *qtd. in.*

    CMOS: (quoted in Smith 2017)
    APA: (Smith, 2017, as cited in Jones, 2019)
    MLA: (qtd. in Smith 110)

Works Cited Section:
Place the source information for each in-text citation in the
"Works Cited" or "Reference List" section at the end of the
document. List sources alphabetically by author's last name.

Begin the first line of each source at the left margin, and indent
any runover a half inch. Do not insert a space between
sources. Each style guide arranges two or more sources from
the same author(s) differently:

- **CMOS**. Use a 3-em dash (———) in place of the
  author's name with subsequent sources. Arrange
  sources chronologically with "n.d." (no date) sources
  last. Alphabetize sources with the same date by title.
- **APA**. Repeat the author's name with each source.
  Arrange sources chronologically with "n.d." first.
  Alphabetize sources with the same date by title.
- **MLA**. Use three hyphens (---) in place of the author's
  name with subsequent sources. Arrange sources
  alphabetically by title.

Works Cited Example (CMOS Format):

Henley, Greta. 2004. *Grammar: A Reference for Teachers*. New York: Penguin.

Wick, Kenneth. 2012. *The Court Reporter's Reference of Commonly Used Words and Phrases*. CreateSpace.

————. 2019a. *The Essential 99 Punctuation Rules for Court Reporters: Reference Edition*. Amazon.

————. 2019b. *The Essential 99 Punctuation Rules for Court Reporters: Workbook*. Amazon.

————. n.d. *The Court Reporter's Reference of Realtime Conflicts*, 2nd ed. CreateSpace.

Zimmerman, Audrey. 2003. *The Economics of Education*. Cambridge: Cambridge University Press.

Reference List Example (APA Format):

Henley, G. (2004). *Grammar: A Reference for Teachers*. Penguin.

Wick, K. (n.d.). *The Court Reporter's Reference of Realtime Conflicts* (2nd ed). CreateSpace.

Wick, K. (2012). *The Court Reporter's Reference of Commonly Used Words and Phrases*. CreateSpace.

Wick, K. (2019a). *The Essential 99 Punctuation Rules for Court Reporters: Reference Edition*. Amazon.

Wick, K. (2019b). *The Essential 99 Punctuation Rules for Court Reporters: Workbook*. Amazon.

Zimmerman, A. (2003). *The Economics of Education*. Cambridge University Press.

Works Cited Example (MLA Format):

Henley, Greta. *Grammar: A Reference for Teachers*. Penguin, 2004.

Wick, Kenneth. *The Court Reporter's Reference of Commonly Used Words and Phrases*. CreateSpace, 2012.

---. *The Court Reporter's Reference of Realtime Conflicts*. 2nd ed., CreateSpace, n.d.

---. *The Essential 99 Punctuation Rules for Court Reporters: Reference Edition*. Amazon, 2019.

---. *The Essential 99 Punctuation Rules for Court Reporters: Workbook*. Amazon, 2019.

Zimmerman, Audrey. *The Economics of Education*. Cambridge UP, 2003.

Four things are needed to create a source citation:

- Author's name
- Publication date
- Work title
- Publication details

The necessary publication details depend on the source type. Therefore, record all publication details that apply.

- **Book**. Publisher, city of publication, editor, translator, edition number, volume number, page numbers, repository location, and DOI/URL.
- **Book Chapter**. Book title, book author, publisher, city of publication, editor, translator, edition number, volume number, page numbers, repository location, and DOI/URL.
- **Journal** or **Magazine**. Journal or magazine name, volume number, issue number, publication date, page numbers, repository location, and DOI/URL.
- **Newspaper**. Newspaper name, publication date, starting page number, repository location, and DOI/URL.
- **Web Page**. Website name, URL, and access date.
- **Lecture** or **Presentation**. Event name, event location (venue, city, and state), slide number, time marker (hour-minute-second format), and DOI/URL.
- **Audiovisual**. Director, host production company or organization, media type or format (film, DVD), catalog number, supplemental recording or performance information, time marker (hour-minute-second format), and DOI/URL.

Online Sources:
A source consulted online must include a DOI (digital object identifier) or a URL (uniform resource locator) to the source. If the source is in a commercial database (paid access), provide a link to the database or the source's information page. Refer to pages 139 and 140 for information about online sources with no publication date, inserting a line break into a URL, and shortening a long URL.

Repository Location:
For a source with limited access, place the repository information (address, call number) as a note in the citation.

Work with Two Authors:
    CMOS: Smith, John, and Robert Jones
    APA: Smith, J. & Jones, R.
    MLA: Smith, John, and Robert Jones

Work with Three Authors:
    CMOS: Smith, John, Robert Jones, and Emma Williams
    APA: Smith, J., Jones, R., & Williams, E.
    MLA: Smith, John, et al.

Work with Four or More Authors:

    CMOS: List all authors.

    APA: List up to twenty authors. For twenty-one or
             more authors, list the first nineteen authors,
             insert an ellipsis (. . .), and list the final
             author without a preceding ampersand (&).

    MLA: Smith, John, et al.

Publication Date:
Use "n.d." when the source has no publication date.

    CMOS: 2017
             2019a
             2019b
             (1813) 2003

             When the original publication date is
             important, place it before the republication
             date in parentheses. When the date is not
             important, include it at the end of the source
             ("Original published in 1813").

    APA: (2016)
             (2017a, June 4)
             (2017b, Fall)

             For a republished work, include the original
             publication date at the end of the source
             ("Original work published in 1813").

    MLA: 2020
             Dec. 2020
             14 Jan. 2018

             Use a day-month-year format with
             abbreviated months using a period (Rule 77).

Work Title:

    CMOS: Capitalize the title per Rule 64. Italicize the title of a book, journal, magazine, or website. Enclose the title of a book chapter, journal or magazine article, or web page in quotation marks (Rule 35 and Rule 58).

    APA: Only capitalize the first word and words normally capitalized, like proper nouns. Italicize the title of a book, journal, magazine, or website. Do not enclose the title of a book chapter, journal or magazine article, or web page in quotation marks.

    MLA: Same as CMOS.

Book (Basic Format):

    CMOS: Smith, Martin. 2001. *Essential Grammar*. Chicago: Random House.

    APA: Smith, M. (2001). *Essential grammar*. Random House.

    MLA: Smith, Martin. *Essential Grammar*. Random House, 2001.

Book with Editor or Translator:

    CMOS: Smith, Martin. 2001. *Essential Grammar*. Edited by Allison Jones. Chicago: Random House.

    APA: Smith, M. (2001). *Essential grammar* (A. Jones, Editor). Random House.

    MLA: Smith, Martin. *Essential Grammar*. Edited by Allison Jones. Random House, 2001.

Book with Edition or Volume:

    CMOS: Smith, Martin. 2001. *Essential Grammar*, 2nd ed., Vol. 2. Chicago: Random House.

    APA: Smith, M. (2001). *Essential grammar* (2nd Ed., Vol. 4). Random House.

    MLA: Smith, Martin. *Essential Grammar*. 2nd ed., vol. 4, Random House, 2001.

Book Consulted Online:
Provide a DOI (preferred) or URL to the source. If the source is in a commercial database (paid access), provide a link to the database or an information page. For MLA style, the "http://" or "https://" in a URL may be omitted.

CMOS: Smith, Martin. 2001. *Essential Grammar*. Chicago: Random House. https://doi.org/10.1234/8080

APA: Smith, M. (2001). *Essential grammar*. Random House. https://doi.org/10.1234/8080

MLA: Smith, Martin. *Essential Grammar*. Random House, 2001. https://doi:10.1234/8080.

Chapter from a Book:

CMOS: Smith, Leah. 2015. "Common Comma Errors." In *English Punctuation*, 2nd ed., edited by Robin Jones, 112–128. New York: Penguin Press.

APA: Smith, L. (2015). Common comma errors. In R. Jones (Ed.), *English punctuation* (2nd ed., pp. 112–128). Penguin Press.

MLA: Smith, Leah. "Common Comma Errors." *English Punctuation*, edited by Robin Jones. 2nd ed., Penguin Press, 2015, pp. 112–128.

Journal Article (Basic Format):

CMOS: Smith, John. 2005. "The Exclamation Mark." *Grammar Quarterly* 5, no. 2 (March 2005): 5–8.

A colon always precedes page numbers. If no date, place the issue number in parentheses: *Grammar Quarterly* 5 (2): 5–8.

APA: Smith J. (2005). The exclamation mark. *Grammar Quarterly*, 5(2), 5–8.

MLA: Smith, John. "The Exclamation Mark." *Grammar Quarterly*, vol. 5, no. 2, March 2005, pp. 5–8.

Journal Article Consulted Online.
See comments about web links in "Book Consulted Online*."*

> CMOS: Jones, Linda. 2019. "The Exclamation Mark
> Revisited." *Grammar Quarterly* 19, no.3
> (Fall):   11–14.   https://www.grquarterly.
> com/journal/19-3/exclamation-mark-revisited.

> APA: Jones, L. (2019). The exclamation mark
> revisited. *Grammar Quarterly*, 19(3), 11–
> 14. https://www.grquarterly.com/journal/19-3
> /exclamation-mark-revisited.

> MLA: Jones, Linda. "The Exclamation Mark
> Revisited." *Grammar Quarterly*, vol. 19,
> no.3, Fall 2019, pp. 11–14. *Grammar
> Quarterly*, www.grquarterly.com/journal/19-3
> /exclamation-mark-revisited.

Newspaper or Magazine Article:
Format a magazine article containing volume and issue
information like a journal article. Include a web link if the article
was accessed online (see "Book Consulted Online").

> CMOS: Rodriguez, Angelina. 2017. "Practical
> Sentences." *The New York Times*,
> October 28, 2017, C5.

> APA: Rodriguez, A. (2017, October 28). Practical
> sentences. *The New York Times*, C5.

> MLA: Rodriguez, Angelina. "Practical Sentences."
> *The New York Times*, 28 Oct. 2017, p. C5.

Web Page:
When an online source has no publication date, an access
date must be included in the source.

> CMOS: Jones, Wendy. 2020. "Writing Reports."
> *Grammar Quarterly*. Published July 21, 2020.
> https://www.grquarterly.com/resources
> /wr-reports.
>
> Nunes. Victor. n.d. "Outlining." *Grammar
> Quarterly*. Accessed February 16, 2020.
> https://www.grquarterly.com/resources
> /outlining."

APA: Jones, Wendy. (2020, July 21). Writing reports. *Grammar Quarterly*. https://www.grquarterly.com/resources/wr-reports.

Nunes. Victor. (n.d.). Outlining. *Grammar Quarterly*. Retrieved February 16, 2020, from https://www.grquarterly.com/resources/outlining.

MLA: Jones, Wendy. "Writing Reports." *Grammar Quarterly*, 21 July 2020, www.grquarterly.com/resources/wr-reports.

Nunes. Victor. "Outlining." *Grammar Quarterly*, www.grquarterly.com/resources/outlining. Accessed 16 Feb. 2020.

Lecture or Presentation:

CMOS: Jones, William. 2017. "The Direction of Capitalization." The 4th Annual Grammar Convention, New York, December 10, 2017.

APA: Jones, W. (2017, December 10). The direction of capitalization. The 4th Annual Grammar Convention, New York.

MLA: Jones, William. "The Direction of Capitalization." The 4th Annual Grammar Convention, 10 Dec. 2017, New York.

Audiovisual:

Include relevant supplemental information: media type or format, catalog number, production or performance information, or time marker to a specific part (hour-minute-second format). Provide DOI or URL if accessed online.

Film:

CMOS: Forman, Milos, dir. 1975. *One Flew Over the Cuckoo's Nest*. Los Angeles: United Artists. Film.

APA: Forman, M. (Director). (1975). *One flew over the cuckoo's nest* [Film]. United Artists.

MLA: *One Flew Over the Cuckoo's Nest*. Directed by Milos Forman. United Artists, 1975.

Web Video:

CMOS: Clark, Mary, host. 2003. "Practical Grammar." University of English, August 23, 2003. Video. https://youtube.com/923u03h.

APA: Clark, M. (Host). (2003). Practical grammar [Video]. University of English. https://youtube.com/923u03h

MLA: Clark, Mary, host. "Practical Grammar." University of English, 23 August 2003. *YouTube*, youtube.com/923u03h.

Music Album:

CMOS: Bowie, David. 2016. *Blackstar*. Columbia Records, compact disc.

APA: Bowie, D. (2016). *Blackstar* [Album]. Columbia Records.

MLA: Bowie, David. *Blackstar*. Columbia Records, 2013.

Song:

CMOS: Beyoncé, 2016. "Pretty Hurts." *Beyoncé*, Columbia Records, compact disc, https://www.beyonce.com/album/beyonce/songs.

APA: Beyoncé, (2016). Pretty hurts [Song]. On *Beyoncé*, Columbia Records. https://www. beyonce.com/album/beyonce/songs.

MLA: Beyoncé, "Pretty Hurts." *Beyoncé*, Columbia Records, 2013, www.beyonce.com/album /beyonce/songs.

www.ingramcontent.com/pod-product-compliance
Lightning Source LLC
Chambersburg PA
CBHW061759250726
48657CB00001B/192